THE LIFESTYLE OF JESUS

LIVING A FULFILLING & PRODUCTIVE LIFE IN THE 21st CENTURY

Wendell P. Karsen

To: Harvey & Margaret Doorenbos
Blessings
Wendell Karsen
August 2016

AMAZON CREATE SPACE

AMAZON CREATE SPACE

Copyright ©2016 by Wendell P. Karsen

All rights reserved. No part of this publication may be reproduced, stored in a retrieval system, or transmitted in any form or by any means, electronic, mechanical, photocopying, recording, or otherwise, without the prior permission of the author.
Printed in the United States of America

GNT All scripture quotations in this publication are from the Good News Translation in Today's English Version-Second Edition, Copyright © 1992 by American Bible Society. All rights reserved. Bible text from the Good News Translation (GNT) is not to be reproduced in copies or otherwise by any means except as permitted in writing by American Bible Society, 101 North Independence Mall East, FL 8, Philadelphia, PA 19106-2155. (www.americanbible.org). Used by Permission.

The illustrations by Swiss artist and storyteller Annie Vallotton, in Chapter Nine are taken from the Good News Translation © 1976, 1992, 2015 American Bible Society and are also used by permission.

The Cover illustration is a painting entitled "The Prince of Peace" by Akiane Kramarik. Copyright © Truthbook. Used by permission.

ISBN number: 10:1530967406
ISBN number: 13:978-1530967407

THE LIFESTYLE OF JESUS

Table of Contents

Preface --- vii

Ready ... Set ... GO! --- ix

Chapter 1 - Who Is Right? -- 1

Chapter 2 - Valuing What Is Valuable ------------------------- 11

Chapter 3 - It's All about Love --------------------------------- 19

Chapter 4 - Who Do You Trust?- -------------------------------- 29

Chapter 5 - Obedience Training --------------------------------- 37

Chapter 6 - Patience Is a Priority ------------------------------- 49

Chapter 7 - Kindness Is the Oil of Life ------------------------ 57

Chapter 8 - The Last Shall Be First! --------------------------- 69

Chapter 9 - Who Cares? -- 81

Chapter 10 - Be Forgiving and Enjoy Living ----------------- 91

Chapter 11 - Are You a Constructive Person? ---------------103

Chapter 12 - A Cure for Cowardice --------------------------- 111

Chapter 13 - Honesty *Is* the Best Policy ---------------------- 123

Chapter 14 - You Forgot to Say "Thank You" -------------- 133

Chapter 15 - How Is 'Freedom' Spelled? --------------------- 143

Chapter 16 - All the World's a Stage --------------------------- 153

Chapter 17 - Use What You've Got! ---------------------------161

Chapter 18 - Is 'Repentance' Out of Date? -------------------- 172

Chapter 19 - A Formula for Joyful Living -------------------- 183

Chapter 20 - Is Peace Possible? -------------------------------- 193

You Take It from Here --------------------------------------- 202

Preface

The Lifestyle of Jesus grew out of a course that was conceived at Ying Wa College in Hong Kong and developed and refined there over a three year period. During that time, it was gratifying to see the interest shown in it by my students and the positive development that took place in many of their lives. They responded well to an approach that emphasized personal interaction with Jesus' ideas rather than mere assimilation of information about him. They appreciated the relevance of those ideas for their lives and situations today. And in the process, they became more and more open to seriously thinking about becoming his followers and adopting his lifestyle as their own.

Towards the end of each year, I assigned an essay. The students could choose one of the following topics:

1. "Why I am a follower of Jesus Christ."

2. "Why I am not a follower of Jesus Christ."

3. "Why I have not yet decided about becoming a follower of Jesus Christ."

The essays of a great majority of the students showed that a lot of in depth thinking had been going on throughout the year and that significant things had happened in their lives.

These students were a delight to teach. They had a real desire to do some serious thinking about life, to sort out their beliefs, values and priorities and to commit themselves to something. And they had developed the mental and emotional maturity that's required to begin to do this. I would be surprised if there weren't a good number of such people in the crowds that heard Jesus gladly long ago (the boy with the five rolls and two fish, for example?). And I think they're just as glad to hear him today, provided that through what they read and hear, they can hear him clearly.

I am indebted to my (now deceased) first wife, Joyce, and to my children for their constant encouragement and understanding during those days. Most of all, however, I would like to thank my students at Ying Wa College, to whom this book is dedicated. Without them, this book would never have seen the light of day. With them, I was able to write it. During the process, I'm sure they taught me as much as I taught them. My prayer for them is that as they have moved on to places of responsibility in Hong Kong society, they will continue to live out the lifestyle of Jesus.

Retirement has now given me the opportunity to re-write, expand, contextualize and refine the material in this book. My hope is that it will prove to be helpful to all who are trying to wend their way through the complexities of life today and would like to do so in the style that Jesus modeled for the world so long ago.

Wendell Paul Karsen
Penney Farms, Florida
May 2016

Introduction

Get Ready, Get Set -------------- Go!

You're off on an adventure to discover more about yourself and to work at developing a more meaningful lifestyle. As you 'run' through this book, promise yourself right now that you'll make a serious effort to diligently work through the material presented and to honestly consider whatever new ideas might come your way.

Working out a wholesome lifestyle in today's world is no easy matter. Your peers have some pretty strong ideas about the way they've gone about living and the way in which *you* should live. So do your family, your colleagues and your friends. And then there are the people in the movies you see, the magazines you read, the music you listen to, the sports you follow, the television you watch, the Internet you surf, the books you devour - and all the rest. Confusing, isn't it? So many people living so many different lifestyles, acting in such different ways, believing such different things - all calling on *you* to join them.

The purpose of this book is to help you cut through this confusion by considering a number of ideas about life that have stood the test of time and that have brought meaning and purpose to the lives of many. They come from an exciting person who knew a lot about life and who came to this world long ago to make it possible for people to live life fully and freely. As you interact with these ideas and this person, perhaps you'll discover that 'the lifestyle of Jesus' is for you. If you've already made that discovery, perhaps this book will help deepen your commitment to him and to his way of life.

Now that you're off, run a good race through this book. See you again when you get to the finish line on the last page.

Chapter One

WHO IS RIGHT?

> **Read All About It!**
>
> Read how a smart man changed his mind about the TRUTH in Acts 9:1-22.

What Is Truth?

It's a confusing world. Our parents tell us one thing, our friends tell us another. The newspaper columnist argues for 'A' today, the T. V. commentator argues for 'B' tomorrow. One colleague favors this, another favors that. Who's right? What *is* the truth? How can we decide? The following are brief descriptions of some major philosophical positions. Which position(s) do you feel most describe(s) your present view of reality?

Hedonism teaches that pleasure or happiness alone is the supreme good. All human motivation is the desire to avoid pain and gain pleasure.

Nihilism denies the existence of reality, knowledge or values. We can know nothing for sure.

Mysticism teaches that knowledge of reality can't be had through logical or scientific means, but only through immediate awareness of that which is to be known.

Materialism holds that reality (even the mind and consciousness) is ultimately composed of physical matter. The universe is entirely governed by the physical laws of motion and energy.

Humanism places its emphasis upon human interests and values. Humans are the measure of their own existence. They alone will determine their fate and future without 'God.'

Determinism teaches that all events of the present and future are necessarily as they are and will be because of past causes. The universe is governed entirely by causal laws.

Empiricism maintains that all knowledge comes from experience. All true ideas are based on data gathered by experience and all true facts must be verified by experience.

Rationalism teaches that all ideas are established by deduction. What is felt or experienced can't be true if it's illogical.

Intuitionism opposes empiricism and rationalism by teaching that all true knowledge is based upon intuition rather than being proved by experience or figured out by logic. A person knows truth directly.

Utilitarianism is the view that the good is that which produces the greatest happiness for the greatest number of people. Nothing is therefore good or bad in itself.

Relativism holds that there is no objective standard by which truth may be determined, so that truth varies with individuals and circumstances. There are no such things as absolutes.

Realism is the theory that things exist independently of being known. Universals really exist and are applicable to all people at all time's in all places under all circumstances.

Solipsism maintains that the individual is the whole of reality and that all other entities are simply products of that person's mental operations. The world therefore has no existence independently of that person.

Naturalism teaches that the universe is explainable only in terms of itself. There's no greater reality or force or cause outside of the universe itself.

Confusing isn't it? Would you believe that there are still 23 more basic philosophical systems that have not been described above! *Is* there such a thing as 'truth?' If there is, can we know it? If we can, *how* can we know it? How would *you* go about finding the answers to these questions?

Christians believe that truth is that which corresponds to what has been, is, or must be real for all people at all times in all places. It's important to carefully decide what's true since there are many conflicting viewpoints that all claim to be true and since following what's false will lead to difficulties. If we know and follow the truth, we'll be freed from the anxiety of wondering what's really true and from the difficulties caused by following what's false. (See John 8:32)

Which brings up the question, how can we discern what's true and what's false, who's a true prophet and who's a false prophet?

We can help to determine whether something is true or false by asking:

1. Does it fit reality? For example, you know that it's raining because your clothes are getting wet.

2. Does it match experience? For example, you know that a new airplane design will really work only by performing a test flight.

3. Does it agree with the opinion of trustworthy experts in the area under question? For example, you know that you've cracked a bone when a trained medical doctor examines you, takes an x-ray and tells you that your bone is cracked.

4. Do people I trust believe it's true? For example, when you were a child, your parents told you that stealing was wrong and you believed them.

5. Do a large number of people believe it's true? For example, hardly anybody still believes that the earth is flat.

6. Does it apply to all people everywhere at all times? For example, it's universally true that precipitation will turn into snow if the temperature drops below 32°C.

7. Does it make people more or less human? For example, Adolph Hitler's policy of exterminating the Jews in

World War II can be condemned as false because it devalued and destroyed human beings.

Of course, we can never absolutely, 100%, prove *anything* to be true or false (except for this statement). This is different than saying that there *is* nothing that's true or false. We can't decide what's true on the basis of 'facts,' but only on the basis of *probabilities* (what most *appears* to be true), since we often get fooled by what appear to us as 'facts.' For example, a good magician can create illusions of what *seems* to be true, but we all know that even though we can't prove it at the time, those illusions are just that.

We also know that seeing things with the naked eye and seeing them through a microscope are two different things. What *appears* to be something to the naked eye turns out to be something quite different when viewed through a microscope. We also know that if we look at a straight set of railroad tracks, they will seem to merge in the distance, but when we walk down the tracks, they never do. Therefore, we choose to believe something is true not because to do so causes us no problems, but because to do so causes us the *least number* of problems.

Since nothing is 100% provable, therefore everyone has a certain amount of faith. Something may be able to be 99.999% 'proved,' but the remaining .001% must be believed. Everyone exercises a certain amount of faith in deciding and acting on anything, whether consciously or sub-consciously. For example, getting on a bus is an act of faith. We may not, for a number of reasons, make it to our destination. The bus may have an accident. The driver might have a heart attack or a stroke. The bus might be blown up by a terrorist. The bus might miss our stop. Nevertheless, we still get on the bus since we *believe*, on the basis of probability, that the bus that has gotten us to our destination many times before will do so again.

When it comes to knowing the truth about God, a theist can't prove the existence of God, but neither can an atheist prove the non-existence of God. Therefore, *both* positions require faith. The question then becomes - what's more probable and least problematical when faced with the evidence that God exists or that he doesn't exist? The trend in modern studies is toward increasing the probabilities for the existence of God. The result is that the atheistic and even the agnostic (one who believes there *might* be a God, but who can't be sure) positions are becoming less and less probable and are requiring more and more faith, while the theistic position is becoming more and more probable and is requiring less and less faith.

People usually approach the search for truth in two ways:

Some are open to honestly consider all the evidence and make a great effort to carefully examine it. For example, even though it was difficult and maybe even dangerous, a Jewish leader named Nicodemus came to Jesus after dark in private to ask him about his teaching. In the end, he became a believer and a brave follower of Jesus. (See John 3:1-18; 7:45-52; 19:38-42).

Others either approach the evidence with their minds already made up to reject it or are too lazy to consider it. For example, the elite religious people of Jesus' day, the Pharisees, watched Jesus raise Lazarus from the dead --- and then went and made plans to kill him! (See John 11:45-53) The Jewish chief priests, the teachers of the Law and the elders also saw and heard much of what Jesus did and taught, but stood at the foot of his cross and mocked him saying, "He saved others, but he cannot save himself! Isn't he the king of Israel? If he will come down off the cross now, we will believe in him! He trusts in God and claims to be God's Son. Well, then, let us see if God wants to save him now!" (See Matthew 27:42). (See also John 3:16-21 and Luke 16:27-31)

The Lifestyle of Jesus

Christians believe the final test of truth is whether or not something agrees with the ideas of Jesus who claimed to be *the* truth. "I am the way, the TRUTH and the life," he said. (See John 1:14, 17; 14:6; 18:37). If our human reasoning is the final reference, then there's no way to decide what's true since there are so many conflicting claims to truth. Either Jesus is the reference point for determining what's true or false, or he was the world's greatest liar.

Christians believe the evidence suggests that the probabilities that Jesus really was who he said he was and that he really did what he said he had come to do are much greater than that he wasn't or that he didn't. He passes all the tests mentioned above. Therefore, we can believe that his claims are true.

1. He was a real historical person who lived in Palestine from c. 4 B.C. – 30 A.D. There is more historical proof for his life and ministry than for many prominent historical characters of his era, like Julius Caesar, for example.

2. Millions of people have testified down through the centuries that they've had a life-changing experience by opening their lives to the presence and power of the risen Christ through his Spirit.

3. Hundreds of respected scholars have studied the life and work of Jesus Christ and concluded that he really was who he claimed to be and that he really did what he claimed to do.

4. Millions of Christians have become so because of the testimony of loved ones, friends, neighbors and colleagues who have experienced the forgiveness and

fulfilling new life that Jesus promised to those who become his followers.

5. Of the 6.9 billion people on Earth, there are 2.2 billion who believe in Jesus Christ as their Lord and Savior.

6. People of all races, ages, gender, cultural and ethnic backgrounds and economic and educational status belong to the world-wide Christian Church. As the Apostle Paul wrote to the Christians at Galatia, "There is no difference between Jews and Gentiles, between slaves and free people, between men and women; you are all one in union with Christ Jesus." Galatians 3:28

7. The teaching and example of Jesus Christ have been acknowledged by a great majority of the world's peoples as lifting humanity to its highest aspirations and most fulfilling way of life.

Thinking It Through

Everybody believes certain things to be true and certain things to be false. However, many people never take the time to seriously think about what they believe and why they believe it. They live life from day to day assuming a lot, but seldom think through or test out those assumptions. As a result, they're like a person in a canoe rushing through the rapids of life without a paddle! They aren't really sure about who they are, where they've come from, why they're here and where they're going.

Life under those circumstances can be pretty rough! What about you? Have *you* thought through what you believe to be true and *why* you believe it? Take a piece of paper and try to write out your personal 'creed' about the subjects listed below.

Describe your belief about each item and why you believe what you do. Try to think through your responses carefully enough to limit yourself to a few key sentences for each item.

1. What I believe about the world and why.

2. What I believe about myself and why.

3. What I believe about people and why.

4. What I believe about right and wrong and why.

5. What I believe about the purpose of life and why.

6. What I believe about God and why.

7. What I believe about love and why.

8. What I believe about _____ (fill in yourself) and why.

What Does This Tell You about Yourself?

1. It was easy/difficult for me to write out my personal creed because …..

2. When I think about what I believe, I …..

3. When it comes to my beliefs, I'm still unclear about …..

4. In the future, I would like to believe …..

Chapter Two

VALUING WHAT IS VALUABLE

> **Read All About It!**
>
> Read about what's really VALUABLE in Colossians 3:1-17.

Identifying What Is Valuable

I stared at the paper. The professor's voice droned on, 'Please indicate the 10 items that are most important to you by putting a + next to them. Then indicate the 10 that are least important to you by putting a 0 next to them.'

"I looked at the paper again. A list of 30 items stared back at me, each one of them seeming to say, "Choose me! Choose me!" What would I choose? What's important to me anyway?

"With a start I realized that I hadn't thought about that question very much. I'd sort of drifted along through childhood accepting that this was good or that was bad, this was important or that was silly, this was valuable or that was worthless, because my Mother or Father or Grandmother or brother or teacher or somebody had said it was. Now *I* was being asked not what my Mother or Father or the rest of them thought was important in life, but what *I* thought was important.

"I scanned through the list, my eye pausing on the item 'athletic ability.' My mind wandered. Suddenly I was on the field of my college stadium running like mad towards the distant goal, faking my way through the whole opposing soccer team. I paused, kicked and sent the ball whistling into the net past the outstretched fingertips of the desperate goalie. The whistle blew! The crowd went wild! We had won! And I was the hero!

"I became aware of the professor looking straight at me with that 'Why haven't you written anything down yet?' look on her face. I quickly looked back at the list. 'Athletic ability' ..... was that really important to me? I decided to pass on that one for the moment.

"The next thing to catch my eye was 'Close friendships.' That was an easy one. Who could get along in life as a lonely island? I put down a +. I also put a plus by 'Close family ties.' Mine weren't all that close, but I wished they were. 'A good job' was another easy one. Who'd want to pick up garbage all his life?

"I came to 'Knowing the truth about God.' God? How could I know the truth about him, if there were such a 'him'? I quickly put down a 0, but then paused. To be honest, I'd heard a good bit about God, but had never really thought about him very seriously. Was it fair to 'zero him out' without knowing a little bit more about what I was doing? I erased the 0.

"Next I came to 'Great personal wealth.' My mind wandered again. I was sitting in the back of my Cadillac being driven to my home in Manhattan. It had been a rat-race of a day, but I had closed a big deal and knew that profits this year would be good. Fighting my way to the top of the business world had given me a few gray hairs at forty, but my house with garden and swimming pool and the money to buy whatever I wanted had made it worth it all.

"Or had they? I was back in the classroom again putting down a 0 for that item. More zeros and plusses followed. Time was running short. As I struggled to decide about the remaining items, I found myself feeling more and, more unprepared to make these kinds of judgments. There was a lot about life that I didn't know enough about yet, and some that I was even confused about, but I felt good about having been forced to attempt these choices. I also felt a new sense of determination to do a lot more thinking about myself, my values and my goals in the future than I'd done in the past."

The Lifestyle of Jesus

Jesus once told two parables describing what being his follower (being a member of the Kingdom of Heaven) is like. In the first one, he said that if somebody happens to find a treasure buried in a field, a smart person will go and buy the field in order to get the treasure. (See Matthew 13:44-45)

In the second one, he said that if somebody happens to find a magnificent pearl for sale, a smart person will sell all that he has and buy that pearl. (Matthew 13:46) What he meant was that sometimes it's worth giving up some common things in life in order to obtain something that's really worth having. Of course, what's most worth having in life is usually the most difficult to obtain. We're forced to make choices due to our limitations of time, talent, resources and the like. We must also know *what* we want and *why* want it if we're to make wise and decisive choices. His point was that being a member of God's family (His Kingdom) is worth giving up whatever might cause us to miss the opportunity.

On another occasion, Jesus met with a young man who asked him a surprising question: "What must I do to inherit eternal life?" This question was surprising because this young man seemed to have everything going for him. He was young and at the prime of his physical and mental potential. He was wealthy and could probably afford to buy almost anything he wanted. At his young age, he was already among the ruling class - he had power. He was obviously a well-educated person. He was also a moral person, and therefore a good example to those around him since, when Jesus answered his question by saying that he should keep the Ten Commandments (see Exodus 20:1-17), he replied that he had kept those since he was a boy. However, even though this young man *had* everything anybody could want and *was* what anybody would like to be, he still felt empty inside. His life somehow wasn't very fulfilling.

Jesus then says something that shocks him. "Go, sell all that you have, give it to the poor and come, follow me." Why would he say such a radical thing? Because he could see into the young man's heart and knew that he hadn't really kept *all* the commandments as he said he had. He had missed the last one, the one about having one's life so wrapped around things that the most important things in this life and in the life to come are being neglected.

In other words, Jesus was pointing out that the most important thing in life is to be free to follow the lifestyle of Jesus; that is, to have eternal life. This life is a life made meaningful by one's right relationship with God through becoming a follower of Jesus - a life that begins in this life and continues on throughout the life to come. On the one hand, this means that people will be free of the desire to have more than they need and that they will not make wealth and goods the be all and end all of their lives. On the other hand, this means that, like the rich young ruler, people can have what most people value (wealth, prestige, education, youthful vigor, power, etc.), but still feel they lack what's most important in life.

Jesus doesn't mean, of course, that a person shouldn't acquire riches, power, a good education and the like, but that these things should not be the goal of life or hoarded, but used for the common good.

This story doesn't have a happy ending. The young man sees Jesus' point, but he can't bring himself to free himself from what's so unsatisfying in his life and to begin to live the lifestyle of Jesus. Sadly, he walks away, and in so doing chooses to merely keep on existing rather than truly living. (See Matthew 19:16-26)

On another occasion, Jesus told a story about another wealthy and powerful man. This man owned a large farm and had been very successful - so successful that he didn't know what to do with all the surplus grain his fields produced. Rather than give it to the poor or lower his prices and raise the wages of his workers, he decided to build bigger and bigger barns in order to hoard it and get the maximum profits from it so that he could live in luxury and enjoy 'the good life' for years to come. Jesus calls him a fool, and the punch line of the story is: "You're going to die tonight and then who will get all these things you have kept for yourself? This is how it is with those who pile up riches for themselves but are not rich in God's sight." (See Luke 12:13-31)

The point of the story was, of course, that a person's true life is not made up of the things s/he owns but of the quality of his or her relationships with God and others. Things are temporary, true life is eternal. To live for the former is to lose the latter.

(See Matthew 6:24) In the end, a person's circumstances and destiny do not ultimately lie within her or his power to control. This truth either drives people to the worry of fate ("I'm in the hands of chance") or to the confidence of faith ("Nothing in all creation will be able to separate us from the love of God which is ours through Christ Jesus.") (Romans 8:39)

Jesus then went on to address the crowds of mostly poor people who were listening to him. He pointed out that the poor may be even more tempted than the rich to center their lives around things - things that they don't at present have, but things that they wish they did have. He challenged them to believe that those who are free to live the lifestyle of Jesus (who are concerned with God's Kingdom and its values) can be confident that their basic needs will be supplied. (See Luke 12:22-34)

Thinking It Through

1. If you had to suddenly evacuate your house because of a flood, what would be the first five things you would try to save and why?

2. Take a sheet of paper and write down the twelve things you most enjoy doing in life.

    a. Circle the five things in your list that are most important to you and number them in the order of your preference.

    b. Put an 'A' beside those things you like to do alone and a 'B' beside those things you enjoy doing with others.

    c. Put a dollar sign beside any activity that costs more than $25.00 to do.

d. Put a '52' beside anything you would want to do at least once each week for the rest of your life.

e. Put an 'R' beside an activity that you consider to be a means of relaxation.

f. Put an 'E' beside any activity that involves physical exercise.

g. Put an 'S' beside any activity that involves your spiritual life.

h. Put a 'C' beside any activity you feel challenges you or stretches you to change, grow and develop as a person.

i. Put an 'M' beside any activity you feel gives meaning and purpose to your life.

j. Write down the number of weeks beside each activity that indicates how long it's been since you last did that activity.

What Does This Tell You about Yourself?

1. "I've discovered that I ……………..

2. "I'm surprised that I ………….…….

3. "I'm disappointed that I ……………

4. "I've learned that I need to …………

Chapter Three

IT'S ALL ABOUT LOVE

> ### Read All About It!
>
> Read what real LOVE is like in I Corinthians 13.

What Do We Mean by 'Love'?

When you watch television, surf the Internet, or read newspapers and magazines, you will soon discover that 'love' is *the* favorite subject of the human race.

- ❖ A protester holds up a sign …. "Make *LOVE*, not WAR!"
- ❖ A song blasts out over the radio …. "Love is a many splendored thing."
- ❖ A soldier's tombstone conveys the somber message …. "He loved his country."
- ❖ A boy walks by with a T-shirt imprinted …. "Love Makes the World Go Round."
- ❖ A Church bulletin board admonishes …. "Love your neighbor as yourself."

- ❖ A theatre marquee lights up the street advertizing …. "The Love story."

- ❖ A book on pets is entitled …. "For All You Animal Lovers."

- ❖ A teenager exclaims …. "I love McDonald's hamburgers!"

- ❖ A real-estate salesman says to a prospective buyer …. "Don't you just love this house?"

- ❖ A philanthropist says …. "I'm making this donation because I love this community."

- ❖ A TV newscast tells of a mother who sacrificed a kidney because …. "I love my son, and without it he will die."

Confusing isn't it? So many different ideas all being expressed through that one little word 'LOVE.' By the way, what usually first comes to *your* mind when you hear the word 'love'? (Think about that for a minute before you read on.) A host of people (if they're honest!) get a little nervous and think about romance. (Have you ever noticed how teenagers giggle when this subject comes up?)

If you did a series of sidewalk interviews and asked people what comes to their mind when they think of the word 'love,' you'd probably get more or less the same answer nine out of ten times - "Romance." Try it sometime. However, from the slogans we're bombarded with on Television, on the Internet, on billboards, in the movies and in newspapers and magazines, we know that even though 'love' is such a small word, it has more than a few big meanings! In fact, if you were to choose one of the slogans above as expressing the basic meaning of the word 'love,' which one would you vote for? Maybe none of them fits your own idea of love very well. How would you define the word 'love'? Now try to form your idea into a slogan that would be good enough to put on a poster or a T-shirt.

A famous teacher once told a story about love that went something like this. "A certain illegal immigrant was attacked by gang members while walking on a back street in Los Angeles. They stripped him and beat him up, leaving him half dead. It so happened that a white Protestant pastor was walking down that street on his way to a meeting of the LA Ministerial Fellowship. He saw the whole thing happen, but because he was late and knew it would be a complicated cultural situation were he to get involved, he hurriedly walked by on the other side of the street

"In the same way, a Catholic priest came by. He stopped, went over and looked at the man. He thought about helping him, but then hesitated because the man was all bloody and dirty and he was headed for his church dressed in a good suit. Besides, people would call him a fool for getting involved in a gang incident involving an illegal immigrant who was a total stranger on a dangerous side street. So he too went on his way without helping the man.

"But a black taxi driver who was driving along that street noticed him lying on the sidewalk, and when he saw the man, his heart was filled with pity. He stopped his taxi, got out and went over to him. He got some water from a nearby water fountain, took out his handkerchief and wiped the blood from the man's face. He then picked the man up, put him into his taxi and took him to the hospital. He took him into the emergency room, and after the man had been admitted, he said to the cashier, "Ask the staff to take good care of him, and when I come back to visit him, I'll try to bring some money to help with the costs."

Who told the original story on which this story is based? (See Luke 10:25-37) What does this story say about love? In all honesty, what would *you* have done in this situation?

The Lifestyle of Jesus

The Greeks had six different words to cover what we in English try to cover in *one* word! Consequently, as we've seen above, our English word 'love' is used in many different ways: romantic love - "I love you;" family love - "He loves his child;" sisterly love - "She loves her friend;" social love - "He loves his hometown;" love of animals - "They love their dog;" philanthropic love - "He loves his hospital project;" love of things - "I love this spaghetti!" aesthetic love - "He loves guitar music;" and self-giving love - "Love your neighbor as yourself."

When Jesus used the word 'love' (as in Matthew 22:36-40), he usually referred to self-giving love. From his point of view, the other uses of the word only became meaningful as they were influenced by this.

What does Jesus mean by self-giving love? How does it express itself in relation to God and our neighbor?

In relation to God, self-giving love expresses itself in obedience and in trust (or faith).

John writes to one of his churches:

> "This is how we know that we love God's children: it is by loving God and obeying his commands. For

our love for God means that we obey his commands. And his commands are not too hard for us, because every child of God is able to defeat the world. And we win the victory over the world by means of our faith. Who can defeat the world? Only the person who believes that Jesus is the Son of God.

By this we know that we love the children of God, when we love God and obey his commandments. For this is the love of God, that we keep his commandments. And his commandments are not burdensome. For everyone who has been born of God overcomes the world. And this is the victory that has overcome the world - our faith. Who is it that overcomes the world except the one who believes that Jesus is the Son of God?" (1 John 5:2-5)

In relation to our neighbor, self-giving love expresses itself in patience, kindness, humility, concern, forgiveness and helpfulness. Paul writes to the Christians at Corinth: "Love is patient and kind; it is not jealous or conceited or proud; love is not ill-mannered or selfish or irritable; love does not keep a record of wrongs; love is not happy with evil, but is happy with the truth. Love never gives up; and its faith, hope, and patience never fail." (1 Corinthians 13:4-7)

Love for God and love for neighbor are interconnected. We can't truly express the one without expressing the other. Love for neighbor is a gift from God; love for God is proved by love for neighbor.

John also writes this to that same church:

> "Dear friends, let us love one another, because love comes from God. Whoever loves is a child of God and knows God. Whoever does not love does not know God, for God is love. And God showed his love for us by sending his only Son into the world, so that we might have life through him. This is what love is: it is not that we have loved God, but that he loved us and sent his Son to be the means by which our sins are forgiven…We love because God first loved us. If we say we love God, but hate others, we are liars. For we cannot love God, whom we have not seen, if we do not love others, whom we have seen. The command that Christ has given us is this: whoever loves God must love others also." (1 John 4:7-11, 19-21)

Thinking It Through

These photos are all sending a message about the meaning of the word 'love.' Study them carefully and then consider the questions below.

It's All About Love

Which of the above photos best expresses your understanding of the meaning of love? Explain.

1. Rank the rest of the photos according to your preference, labeling your second choice #2, your third choice #3, and so on, with the last choice being the photo which you think least expresses your understanding of the meaning of love.

2. Explain why you chose what you did as your last choice.

3. Write a caption under each photo that describes what you think it says about love, with each caption beginning, "Love is ....

4. What photo you can best imagine yourself being in. Why?

Write a Poem

Cinquain is a poetry form that comes from France. The name refers to the French word for the number five.

There are five lines in a Cinquain Poem.

Line 1 - Title (a noun: 1 word)

Line 2 - Describes the title (2 words)

Line 3 - Action words or phrase about the title (3 words)

Line 4 - Describes a feeling about the title (4 words)

Line 5 - Refers to the title (1 word)

Here are some examples.

LOVE

Is Wonderful

Peaceful, Joyful, Kind

Full of New Hope

Needful

FAITH

Is Belief

Confident, Trusting, Loving

Makes Me Become Strong

Wonderful

Now see if you can write a Cinquain Poem about love as you understand it.

What Do These Exercises Tell You about Yourself?

1. "When I think about love, I feel ……………..

2. "If I were to explain my understanding of what love is, I would say that it ….…………..

3. "When Jesus talked about love, I think he meant ……..……..

4. "One way in which I could be more loving would be ……….

Chapter Four

WHO DO YOU TRUST?

> **Read All About It!**
>
> Read about people who really lived out their FAITH in Hebrews 11:1-12:2.

Vignettes of Trust

Jack had been excited about joining the Outward Bound summer camp experience for months. Now that he was there, he wasn't so sure! He looked down at the valley floor far beneath him, closed his eyes and hung on tight. "Don't look down!" a voice shouted from above, "Look up!"

He looked up. The long rope that he was clutching stretched above him in a slender line to his goal at the top of the cliff. Would it hold, he wondered? It must! He sucked in a big breath, gritted his teeth, dug in his heels and slowly inched his way towards the top.

****

Judy had never been in an airplane before. She could hardly believe that she was finally on her way to visit her relatives in Canada. The engines roared; the plane moved swiftly down the runway and then climbed sharply into the sky. As the ground rapidly fell away below, Judy's hands felt a little clammy. She gripped the arms of her seat as she stared out the window. "What if the plane should crash?" she thought. She settled back in her seat and pulled a magazine out of the seat pocket in front of her. "Don't be silly," she said half aloud, "this one will be all right."

****

Cliff bared his arm and looked the other way. The nurse finished her preparations and before he knew what had happened, she had expertly popped the needle into his arm and was pushing down the plunger. With an inward grin, he recalled the scene from the horror movie he'd watched on television the night before where unsuspecting people had been murdered by a mad scientist posing as a country doctor - using injections!

What was the shot he was being given today? He had to confess he really didn't have any idea. The doctor had told him that it would help him to get better, and that had been that. "It's strange," he mused, "how people will put so much confidence in somebody who knows more about something than they do."

****

Linda Patmos had been in Hong Kong for three days. She'd enjoyed shopping and sightseeing and meeting new people. Today, she'd planned a trip up to what the locals called the Peak.' She arrived at the station, paid her fare and got on board.

The tram moved out of the station and began its long, slow climb up the mountain. As the funicular tram car climbed higher and higher, she busied herself with taking pictures of the breathtaking scenery out of the window. About half-way up, they passed a tram coming down the other way. Linda watched as it slowly receded into the distance below. Her eye fell on the cable sliding along on greasy pulleys between the rails. "Two trams full of people depending on that one cable," she thought. "That's a lot of trust!"

****

Phyllis stood at the front of the church looking beautiful in her silk bridal gown. The pastor continued, "I'll now ask you to exchange your vows." Phyllis turned to face the young man she'd grown to love. As he began to repeat his vows after the pastor, she looked into his eyes.

Her mind flitted back to the first time she had looked into those eyes. Then she'd looked questioningly and seen a question mark reflected in his look back at her. After that, they'd slowly grown to know each other and then to love each other, and somehow, somewhere, the question marks had disappeared.

Now, as she looked into his eyes and heard his promises, she knew without a doubt that he would keep them. She knew deep down in her heart that he was making a lifetime commitment to her.

****

These are just a few stories about that common commodity known as 'faith.'

When it comes to relationships, to have faith means that you're willing to trust someone who has shown that s/he deserves your trust, even though you can't be 100% sure of the outcome at the time and even if that outcome might look impossible at the time. We trust people like our parents who've shown themselves to be trustworthy by keeping their promises. We trust people like our doctors who demonstrate that they know more about our health than we do. We trust people like our friends who've been through the thick and thin of life with us and who we know have our best interests at heart.

For example, even though they may have doubts and fears, young children will believe or do what their parents tell them or ask them to do because they've learned to trust them. When a father is teaching his son how to swim, for example, he assures him that he'll hold him up so he won't sink in the water – and the boy trusts him to keep his word.

When a mother promises her daughter that she'll feel much better if she allows the doctor to give her an injection even though it might hurt a bit, her daughter trusts her and tearfully rolls up her sleeve.

The personal experiential bond between parent and child (or in any relationship) is what is crucial in developing trust. A child is, for example, more convinced by experiencing the love and competence of its parents than by hearing explanations from its parents. Its confidence is in a person more than in ideas. Based on that experience, a child will dare to risk all when, for example, the house is on fire, the child is in the upper story window screaming for help and the father is down on the street shouting, "Jump! I'll catch you!" And the child jumps.

The Lifestyle of Jesus

Jesus taught us that one's faith in God should be like a child's trust in its parents. "Let the children come to me, and do not stop them, because the Kingdom of God belongs to such as these. I assure you that whoever does not receive the Kingdom of God like a child will never enter it." (Mark 10: 14-15)

He also asked us to trust him as the Way to the Father. "Whoever believes in me believes not only in me but also in him who sent me. Whoever sees me sees also him who sent me. I have come into the world as light, so that everyone who believes in me should not remain in the darkness." (John 12:44-45)

What has Jesus asked us to trust him for (promised to do for us)?

1. To enable us to know God (who came to us in Jesus). "No one has ever seen God. The only Son, who is the same as God and is at the Father's side, he has made him known." (John 1:18)

2. To enable us to be the kind of people we were intended to be. "I am the light of the world. Whoever follows me will have the light of life and will never walk in darkness." (John 8:12)

3. To enable us to find forgiveness for whatever we are that we shouldn't be or for whatever we've done that we shouldn't have done. "For God loved the world so much that he gave his only Son, so that everyone who believes in him may not die but have eternal life. For God did not send his Son into the world to be its judge, but to be its savior." (John 3:16-17)

4. To enable us to live a meaningful life with right ideas, values, goals and ideals now and in the life to come. "I have come in order that you might have life - life in all its fullness." (John 10:10)

5. To provide us with all that we need for our spiritual lives. "I am the bread of life," Jesus said. "Those who come to me will never be hungry; those who believe in me will never be thirsty... I am the bread of life. Your ancestors ate manna in the desert, but they died. But the bread that comes down from heaven is of such a kind that whoever eats it will not die. I am the living bread that came down from heaven. If you eat this bread, you will live forever." (John 6:11, 48)

6. To enable us to face and overcome difficulties. "Peace is what I leave with you; it is my own peace that I give you. I do not give it as the world does. Do not be worried and upset; do not be afraid...I have told you this so that you will have peace by being united to me. The world will make you suffer. But be brave! I have defeated the world!" (John 14:27; 16:33)

There have been plenty of good teachers down through history. Why should we trust (have faith in) Jesus?

1. Because, as we've seen, he demonstrated that he was who he said he was and that he did what he said he had come to do. He's *reliable*.

2. Because what he taught and the way he lived showed that he knew a lot more than we do about life. He's an *authority*.

3. Because those who have committed their lives to him and his way of life have experienced his love and his power. He can be *known* personally.

What's in the Package?

There are two large identical stamped, addressed, wrapped and tied packages lying on a table in front of you. You don't know what's inside of them. One of them has candy in it, the other just paper and air. You can't really tell which is which without opening one of the packages, but that's against the rules.

- ❖ If a stranger told you the candy was in the package on the right, would you believe him or her? Why or why not?

- ❖ If a friend told you the same thing, would that make any difference? Why or why not?

- ❖ If one of your parents told you the same thing, would that make any difference? Why or why not?

- ❖ If one of your teachers told you the same thing, would that make any difference? Why or why not?

- ❖ If the person who wrapped the packages told you the same thing, would that make any difference? Why or why not?

- ❖ How do you feel about basing your opinion on what someone else says is true?

- ❖ Who are the five people you would most likely believe about things and why?

- ❖ How would you find out for sure if anything was in the package?

What Does This Tell You about Yourself?

1. "It's easy/difficult for me to trust (have faith in) other people's word because ………………

2. "I wish I could ……………………….

3. "I think I can …………………………..

4. The Bible says, "To have faith is to be sure of the things we hope for, to be certain of the things we cannot see." (Hebrews 11:1)

   What are some of the 'things' you think the writer to the Hebrews is talking about here? What is faith in these 'things' based on?

5. "I do / do not/ am not sure I have faith in Jesus because …..

Chapter Five

OBEDIENCE TRAINING

> **Read All About It!**
>
> Read about a disappointing *dis*OBEDIENCE case in Acts 5:17-22.

Sidewalk Interviews

The Scene: an NBC roving reporter is walking around Time Square in New York City with a TV crew doing on-the- spot sidewalk interviews.

NBC Man: "Excuse me a moment. I'm Lester Donahue of NBC. May I ask you a question?"

Lady carrying shopping bag: "I guess so."

Donahue: "I just happened to notice that you waited for the pedestrian light to turn green before you crossed the street... Why did you do that?"

Lady:	"Because if I didn't, I might get killed!"
Donahue:	"That may be, but I noticed a lot of other people who ignored the light and made it across just fine."
Lady:	"Maybe they did, but I think they're foolish. Sooner or later they'll do it once too often and get hurt. That's what happens when you break the law. Besides, they can run faster than I can!"
Donahue:	"Thank you."
	"Hello there, I'm Lester Donahue from NBC. What's your name?"
School Kid:	"I'm Phil Smith."
Donahue:	"I saw you pick up a Coke can lying on the sidewalk and throw it into a garbage can just now. Why did you do that?"
Smith:	"Well, I used to be on one of my school's "Keep New York Clean" teams and I've been very conscious about all the litter lying around ever since. I guess I'm still on a one man crusade against people who are ruining our environment by throwing junk around."
Donahue:	"I see. But a lot of other people don't seem to care all that much."
Smith:	"I know, and that bothers me a lot. People just go around ignoring the law and ignoring

	the welfare of others. People aren't supposed to let their dogs poop on the sidewalk without cleaning it up, for example, but they do it anyway and it makes life less enjoyable for the rest of us."
Donahue:	"I hope our listeners will join your crusade! Thanks a lot."
Tourist in colorful shirt:	"Hello, I'm NBC's roving reporter, Lester Donahue. May I ask you a question?" "Sure. Go ahead."
Donahue:	"How long have you been here in New York?"
Tourist:	"A week and I've really enjoyed it."
Donahue	"Have you gone on any tours, or are you a do-it-yourself kind of tourist?"
Tourist:	"Oh, I've done some things on my own, but I prefer to have a private tour guide show me around. I don't really like group tours all that much because you have to go where the tour guide goes and do what she or he says, but private tour guides know their way around and I don't, so I'm willing to put up with that."
Donahue:	"I see. Well, have a nice time during the rest of your stay here."
Tourist:	"Thanks."

Donahue:	"Hi. I'm Lester Donahue from NBC. What's your name?"
Small boy holding father's hand:	"Aaaa....Johnny Bruggers."
Donahue:	"How old are you Johnny?"
Johnny:	"Six and a half."
Donahue:	"You're getting to be quite a big boy! Let me ask you something. When your Daddy asks you to do something, do you always do it?"
Johnny:	"Most of the time."
Donahue:	"Why?"
Johnny (smiling):	"Because if I don't, I might get a spanking!"
Donahue:	"Suppose your Daddy accidently dropped his wallet into the river here and asked you to jump in after it. Would you do it?"
Johnny (laughing):	"Of course not!"
Donahue:	"Why not?"
Johnny:	"Because my Daddy knows I can't swim very well yet......and he would never ask me to do anything dangerous like that."
Donahue:	"I'm sure he wouldn't, but it's interesting to hear you say that. Thanks for talking with me. Be sure to listen in at 6:00 tonight and you'll be able to see yourself on television!"

****

Go back over the four interviews with Lester Donahue and identify the key sentence in each one that you think says something significant about the idea of obedience.

The Lifestyle of Jesus

When you think about it, who do *you* obey and why? We usually obey those whom we respect because of their knowledge, wisdom and experience. When somebody knows more about something than we do and asks us to do something, we'll usually do it. For example, when a college professor gives the class an assignment, the class obediently does the assignment. They're in the class in the first place because they know the professor knows more than they do and they want to learn.

When somebody who has lived longer than we have and learned a great deal about life gives us advice, we usually take it. For example, when a Christian couple is about to get married, they go to their pastor for marriage counseling. They know that their pastor has been trained to provide such counseling and that s/he has counseled other couples. If the pastor is married, they know that s/he has learned a great deal about marriage and can give wise practical advice to the couple.

When somebody has had a great deal of experience at doing something, we usually do what we're asked to do. For example, in learning how to fly an airplane, a person needs an experienced instructor who has logged the required number of hours to become a flight instructor to teach him or her. We follow what the instructor tells us to do since if we don't, we'll never get the plane off the ground, keep it in the air, or safely land it.

We also learn to obey those who have the power to enforce what they command. For example, when someone enlists in military service, s/he quickly learns that when a sergeant barks a command in boot camp, s/he had better hop to and obey the command or else! When we were children, most of us have had the experience of sitting in the corner for awhile because we failed to obey what our parents asked us to do at one time or another.

We also obey those who love us and who we know have an honest concern for our well-being. For example, children who are dearly loved by their parents and who love them in return will gladly obey them because they know from experience that their parents would never knowingly ask them to do anything that would harm them.

But the greatest motivation for obedience comes from gratitude. When someone expresses their love towards us by giving us a beautiful gift or doing us a great service, we're eager to show our gratitude by doing what that person requests.

These examples all demonstrate that to obey means to actually *do* something, not just to *promise* to do something. Jesus once told a story about two brothers. One made promises but didn't keep them; the other resisted doing what he was asked to do, but in the end, did it. The story goes like this. "Now, what do you think? There was once a man who had two sons. He went to the older one and said, 'Son, go and work in the vineyard today.' 'I don't want to,' he answered, but later he changed his mind and went. Then the father went to the other son and said the same thing. 'Yes, sir,' he answered, but he did not go. Which one of the two did what his father wanted?" "The older one," the crowd answered. (Matthew 21:28-32)

Jesus taught that love towards God expresses itself in an obedience that's willing to freely and cheerfully do what he asks.

> "I love you just as the Father loves me; remain in my love. If you obey my commands, you will remain in my love, just as I have obeyed my Father's commands and remain in his love...My commandment is this: love one another, just as I love you. The greatest love you can have for your friends is to give your life for them. And you are my friends if you do what I command you." (John 15:9-10, 11-14)

Jesus also instructed his followers to teach others to obey what he had commanded them. "Go, then, to all peoples everywhere and make them my disciples: baptize them in the name of the Father, the Son, and the Holy Spirit, and teach them to *obey* everything I have commanded you." (Matthew 28:19-20)

Why do Christians believe that they should obey what Jesus commands?

1. Because of their gratitude for what he did for them. God became the God-man in Jesus in order to bring us forgiveness, a new life in the present and a hope for the future - what the Bible refers to as 'salvation.'

    As Paul puts it,

    > "Now that we have been put right with God through faith, we have peace with God through our Lord Jesus Christ. He has brought us by faith into this experience of God's grace, in which we now live. And so

we boast of the hope we have of sharing God's glory!...For when we were still helpless, Christ died for the wicked at the time that God chose.

"It is a difficult thing for someone to die for a righteous person. It may even be that someone might dare to die for a good person. But God has shown us how much he loves us - it was while we were still sinners that Christ died for us! By his blood we are now put right with God; how much more, then, will we be saved by him from God's anger! We were God's enemies, but he made us his friends through the death of his Son. Now that we are God's friends, how much more will we be saved by Christ's life!" (Romans 5:1-2, 6-10)

2. Because Jesus can be respected for his knowledge, wisdom and experience. The gospel writer Matthew reports, "When Jesus finished saying these things, the crowd was amazed at the way he taught. He wasn't like the teachers of the Law; instead, he taught with authority." (Matthew 7:28)

On another occasion, Jesus was addressing a crowd in the Temple in Jerusalem. John reports that "The Jewish authorities were greatly surprised and said, 'How does this man know so much when he has never been to school?' Jesus answered, 'What I teach is not my own teaching, but it comes from God, who sent me. Whoever is willing to do what God wants will know whether what I teach comes from God or whether I speak on my own authority.'" (John 7:15-17)

On still another occasion, the Jewish Chief Priests sent guards to arrest Jesus. They came back without having arrested him and defended their action by remarking, "Nobody has ever talked the way this man does!" (John 7:45-46)

3. Because Jesus has the authority and the power to enforce what he commands. John reports that Jesus once stormed into the Temple courtyard and drove out all those who were doing business there.

> "It was almost time for the Passover Festival, so Jesus went to Jerusalem. There in the Temple he found people selling cattle, sheep, and pigeons, and also the moneychangers sitting at their tables. So he made a whip from cords and drove all the animals out of the Temple, both the sheep and the cattle; he overturned the tables of the moneychangers and scattered their coins; and he ordered those who sold the pigeons, 'Take them out of here! Stop making my Father's house a marketplace!'" (John 2:13-16)

Once, four men brought a paralyzed man to Jesus on a stretcher. He told the man that his sins were forgiven. Scoffers in the crowd were incensed and accused Jesus of blasphemy. "Only God can forgive sins." Then Jesus said,

> "Why do you think such things? Is it easier to say, 'Your sins are forgiven you,' or to say, 'Get up and walk'? I will prove to you, then, that the Son of Man has authority on earth to forgive sins.' So he said to the

> paralyzed man, 'I tell you, get up, pick up your bed, and go home!'
>
> "At once the man got up in front of them all, took the bed he had been lying on, and went home, praising God. They were all completely amazed! Full of fear, they praised God, saying, 'What marvelous things we have seen today!'" (Luke 5:17-26)

On another occasion, speaking about himself, Jesus said,

> "He who comes from above is greater than all. He who is from the earth belongs to the earth and speaks about earthly matters, but he who comes from heaven is above all. He tells what he has seen and heard, yet no one accepts his message. But whoever accepts his message confirms by this that God is truthful.
>
> "The one whom God has sent speaks God's words, because God gives him the fullness of his Spirit. The Father loves his Son and has put everything in his power. Whoever believes in the Son has eternal life; whoever disobeys the Son will not have life, but will remain under God's punishment." (John 3:31-36)

4. Because Jesus has an honest concern for our well-being. He once said, "I am the good shepherd, who is willing to die for the sheep...As the Father knows me

and I know the Father, in the same way I know my sheep and they know me. And I am willing to die for them." (John 3:11, 17)

What has Jesus asked us to do? He has asked us to freely and cheerfully obey his commandments in a spirit of love. He once said,

> "Do not think that I have come to do away with the Law of Moses and the teachings of the prophets. I have not come to do away with them, but to make their teachings come true. Remember that as long as heaven and earth last, not the least point nor the smallest detail of the Law will be done away with - not until the end of all things.
>
> "So then, whoever disobeys even the least important of the commandments and teaches others to do the same, will be least in the Kingdom of heaven.
>
> On the other hand, "Whoever obeys the Law and teaches others to do the same, will be great in the Kingdom of heaven. I tell you, then, that you will be able to enter the Kingdom of heaven only if you are more faithful than the teachers of the Law and the Pharisees in doing what God requires." (Matthew 5:17-20)

What do Christians believe will be the result of obedience or disobedience to Jesus' commands? According to Jesus,

> "Anyone who hears these words of mine and obeys them is like a wise man who built his house on rock. The rain poured down, the rivers flooded over, and the wind blew hard against that

house. But it did not fall, because it was built on rock.

"But anyone who hears these words of mine and does not obey them is like a foolish man who built his house on sand. The rain poured down, the rivers flooded over, the wind blew hard against that house, and it fell. And what a terrible fall that was!" (Matthew 7:24-27)

In other words, obedience will lead to a stable and wholesome life, while disobedience will lead to disaster and death.

Send a Telegram

Take a piece of paper and pretend that it's a telegram form. Then write a 50 word telegram addressed to your parents telling why you sometimes have (or had) difficulty obeying them.

Write a second one addressed to the Government and a third one addressed to Jesus Christ. Begin each telegram with, "Sometimes I disobey(ed) because …."

What Does This Tell You about Yourself?

1. "I wonder why I have trouble …………...

2. "I wonder what would happen if I were to ……………

3. "I wonder whether I could ……………

4. "I wonder how I would feel if I …………..

Chapter Six

PATIENCE IS A PRIORITY

> **Read All About It!**
>
> Read about PATIENT people in James 5:7-11.

Proverbs about Patience

Here are a number of sayings about the virtue of patience. If you were to explain each one to somebody in one sentence, how would you express the point each is making?

1. "Rome wasn't built in a day."

2. "There's a difference between patience and cowardice."

3. "Rivers know this: there is no hurry. We shall get there someday."

4. "Love is patient."

5. "The greatest oak was once a little nut that held its ground."

6. "Patience and resignation aren't twins."

7. "You can't force a flower to bloom."

8. "Give wind and tide a chance to change."

9. "Patience is a virtue."

10. "The best things in life come to one who waits."

11. "Patience and indifference are not the same thing."

12. "Patience produces positive people."

13. "Water wears down the rock."

14. "The best fruit ripens slowly."

Now see if you can think up a slogan or two of your own about patience.

Puzzles to Try One's Patience

Here are a few puzzles that will try your patience. (The answers are listed at the end of the chapter, but see how long you can hold out without looking at them).

1. Write down five odd figures that will add up to make 14.

2. Place eight eights so that they will add up to a thousand.

3. Demonstrate with ten wooden matches how to take seven-tenths from 'five' so that exactly 'four' remain.

4. Two cyclists race on a circular track. John can around the track in six minutes and Bruce in four minutes. How many minutes will it take Bruce to lap John?

5. There were two people. When you subtracted their ages you got 44. When you multiplied them you got 1,280. How old were they?

The Lifestyle of Jesus

Someone has said, "You should never pray for patience because when you do, God is sure to give you something to try your patience." Someone else has said, "Lord, give me patience - and I want it right now!" Patience is something we're all impatient to have, but as we all know from experience, to have patience is one of the more difficult virtues in life.

The writer of Proverbs says, "It is better to be patient than powerful. It is better to win control over yourself than over whole cities." (Proverbs 16:32) And again, "If you stay calm, you are wise, but if you have a hot temper, you only show how stupid you are. Whoever is patient has great understanding, but one who is quick-tempered displays folly." (Proverbs 14:29)

To live the lifestyle of Jesus, we first of all need patience with ourselves, especially when we fail. Instead of learning from our failures, we can quickly become defeatist and give up trying to become a better person. We know that we're not all that we should be or could be but, as some wag has put it, "Be patient. God isn't through with me yet." There's a lot of truth in that.

The Bible makes it clear that when somebody becomes a Christian, s/he has been 'born again,' meaning that s/he is just beginning a new spiritual journey that will take her or him from spiritual infancy to spiritual maturity. This takes a lot of time and patience, just like it does for a physical new born to get out of diapers, learn how to walk and talk and all the rest. This is what Paul means when he writes to the people of Colossae, "For this reason we have always prayed for you, ever since we heard about you. We ask God to fill you with the knowledge of his will, with all the wisdom and understanding that his Spirit gives. Then you will be able to live as the Lord wants and will always do what pleases him. Your lives will produce all kinds of good deeds, and you will grow in your knowledge of God." (Colossians 1:9-10)

We also need patience with our circumstances, especially when things don't go well. Paul writes to the Christians in Rome, "Be joyful in hope, patient in affliction, faithful in prayer." (Romans 12:12) This was no small request. Christians there were facing hostility and persecution, which would only get worse as time went on. When things aren't going well, it's difficult to patiently endure what must be endured. The temptation is to become bitter or to lose hope. Impatient people are glass-half-empty people. They concentrate on what's wrong and difficult in life. Patient people are glass-half-full people. They concentrate on their blessings, even in the midst of difficulties, and patiently move ahead one day at a time.

We also need patience when it comes to other people. The Peanuts character Linus' most famous comment is, "I love mankind. It's *people* I can't stand!" Getting along with some people is a breeze, but putting up with others is a pain. Paul writes to the Ephesians that the lifestyle of Jesus is to "Be always humble, gentle, and patient. Show your love by being tolerant with one another." (Ephesians 4:2) Notice the word 'always.' That covers those who are easy to get along with and those that are a pain to get along with. Again, a glass-half-empty person will concentrate on other people's faults and follies while a glass-half-full person will concentrate on other people's virtues and achievements.

We also need patience when it comes to God. Especially in times of difficulty, it's all too easy to lose patience with God by asking why this is happening to me and why he doesn't hurry up and do something about it. God always answers our prayers, even those that are prayed with an impatient heart. But he can't always answer, "Yes." For a variety of reasons, oftentimes unknown to us at the moment, he answers, "No" or "Wait" or "I can't right now and you'll understand later."

It's much like parents with children who always want a "Yes" answer and want it right away without often understanding the circumstances. For example, if most kids had their way, they would eat ice cream and candy for breakfast, lunch and dinner, but their parents know what's best for them even though their children wished they didn't. Often, the writers of the Psalms say something like this: "Wait for the Lord; be strong and take heart and wait for the Lord." (Psalm 27:14)

Patience always pays off while impatience gets us into trouble. Sometimes it causes us to give up on what could eventually be beneficial to us. For example, learning to speak a foreign language requires an enormous amount of patience, but is well worth it once a person can begin communicating with people of another culture. At other times, impatience causes us to take things into our own hands with disastrous consequences. For example, in the film *To Kill a Mocking Bird*, rather than allowing a falsely accused black man a fair trial, a gang of bigoted thugs murder him when he makes a run for it and think they're 'enforcing justice.'

At still other times, as we've seen, impatience causes us to become negative – to always complain about the weather or some other temporarily difficult circumstances that can't be changed immediately,

Impatience can also cause us to do things in a hurry with poor results. For example, a student wanting to go to a basketball game rushes through his or her homework and gets a poor grade as a result.

Then too, our impatience can hurt other people and grieve God. For example, a supervisor who gives a worker a hard time even though the worker is trying his or her best gives that worker a feeling of failure and discourages improvement.

The opposite is true, of course, when people live out the lifestyle of Jesus and are patient with themselves, with their circumstances, with their fellow humans and with their God - a patience that is persevering, trusting and hopeful.

How Patient Are You?

1. Think of two occasions when you gave up on something after you failed.

2. Think of two occasions when you lost patience with someone before you should have.

3. Think of two occasions when you became negative and complained when you were faced with circumstances that couldn't be changed immediately.

4. Think of two occasions when you did something in too much of a hurry with poor results.

5. Think of two occasions when you lost patience with God.

6. Think of two occasions when you gave up on something because you thought it was too difficult even though sticking it out could have been beneficial to you.

7. Think of two occasions when you impatiently took things into your own hands with negative consequences.

What Does This Tell You about Yourself?

1. "I've been ....

2. "I need to ....

3. "I find it difficult to ....

4. "I will ....

(Answers to the patience puzzles)

1. 11+1+1+1 = 14.

2. 888+88+8+8+8 = 1,000.

3. Arrange 10 matches this way to spell out the word 'FIVE.'. Then take away the 7 matches forming 'F' and 'E' (seven tenths of the whole) and you leave 'IV', or four.

4. Bruce will lap John in 12 minutes from the start of the race.

5. 64 and 20.

Chapter Seven

KINDNESS IS THE OIL OF LIFE

> ### Read All About It!
>
> Read about a man who was KIND to a potential rival in 2 Samuel 9:1-13.

Kill Them With Kindness!

October 1, 2016

"Dear Ray:

The strangest thing happened in Chicago the other day. We suffered a germ warfare attack! Can you believe it?! You've heard of the war on poverty, the population bomb, the war on terrorism and other types of warfare. Well, some guy went on a "kill them with kindness" rampage here. He apparently went to the Chicago River last Tuesday night and dropped a tiny pill containing some high powered kindness serum he'd developed into the river. It didn't take long before the stuff polluted the whole of Chicago's water supply. The effect was dramatic. It practically turned the whole city on its ear in one day!

"I first noticed it on Thursday morning. When I came down for breakfast, I asked my wife if she would be willing to do an errand for me downtown and she agreed to do it with a smile! I almost fainted. You know how she hates to drive our SUV around in all that traffic. I didn't dare ask her why she was so cheerful about it. I only discovered later that she had just drunk a glass of water.

"The next person to shake me up was the bus driver. Can you believe that he actually waited at the stop for me for a few seconds when he saw me running down the hill like mad? And he smiled too! "What ails this world?" I thought as I sat down. That was another shock. The guy in the aisle seat actually moved over to the middle of a three-seat row so that I didn't have to crawl over his legs. And *he* smiled too! "What's gotten into these people?" I thought. I couldn't resist. I smiled back at him.

"Then I opened my newspaper and I practically dropped it on the floor. There on the front page was a picture of the tycoons of the five biggest companies in Chicago shaking hands with local union leaders! The headline read, "CEOs AGREE TO CUT PROFITS TO GIVE WORKERS A BETTER DEAL!" "This can't be happening in Chicago," I said half aloud….but it was! I couldn't believe it. Of course, little did I realize then that the polluted water supply also had something to do with all this good will.

"When I got to the office, it was simply a different place that day. People went out of their way to do things for each other that they would've complained about or ignored the day before. I was absolutely mystified by it all until I got thirsty, went over to the water cooler, took a drink and joined the fun. I began to suspect that this all had something to do with the water, but that seemed ridiculous. (I heard later that some offices escaped the attack and had a 'normal' day because their water coolers had uncontaminated bottled water in them).

"When I went out for lunch, I noticed that a great change had come over people. The clerk at the Post Office smiled when she gave me my change, and when my string broke, she helped me re-tie my package with some extra string she had lying around. On the way back to the office, people stood patiently in line and didn't rush to get on the bus and grab the empty seats. I also noticed that a policeman was very patient with a homeless man who was partially blocking pedestrian traffic while asking for handouts. He politely asked him to move and helped him find a better spot in the doorway of an abandoned store. Then a student took a blind man by the arm and helped him across a busy street. All kinds of things were going on that I hadn't seen on other days.

"And so it went throughout the day. The more water people drank, the better it became. Nobody knew the water was to blame, of course, until a chemist in a Government Laboratory discovered a strange substance in the water around 4:00 p.m. while doing his normal sampling tests. This caused an uproar at the Water Department. The Government immediately put an emergency water purification plan into action, and, much to everybody's relief, the water was cleaned up overnight.

"By Friday morning, everything was back to normal. It was the usual grousing and "Me first" of any other day. It was actually somewhat of a relief to be acting in the normal way again, knowing what to expect and how to react, and yet, everybody knew the other way was better and had been a lot more fun. In fact, a "Bring Back the Serum" campaign was launched, but the guy who'd dropped the stuff in the river had been arrested and his remaining stock and secret formula had been destroyed. So that was the end of that.

"I can't help thinking about how such a little pill could affect so many people in such a profound way. In my opinion, they ought to let that guy out of prison to see whether he could rediscover that stuff from memory. Life in Chicago may be different, but it's never dull!

Regards,

Bill"

A Little Exercise in Kindness

1. "I've wept in the night for the shortness of sight that to somebody's need made me blind, but I've never yet felt a tinge of regret for being a little too kind."

    Can you write a similar short rhyme about 'kindness'?

2. Take a sheet of paper and spell out the word 'K-I-N-D-N-E-S-S' as an acrostic. Define, explain or elaborate on that word by utilizing each letter of the word to begin one or two horizontal words that, together with the others, form a logical sequence.

Examples

Kindness	**K**indness
Is being	**I**s
Nice	**N**ever
Decent	**D**ancing on the
New every day	**N**erve
Ever	**E**ndings of
Sensitive to every	**S**ensitive
Soul	**S**ouls

The Lifestyle of Jesus

Once Jesus was in a town where there was a man who was suffering from Leprosy. According to Jewish law, he had to wear a sign around his neck saying "UNCLEAN," live outside the town in an isolated place and warn anyone approaching him that he was a leper. In those days, Leprosy was somewhat like Ebola is today. It covered the leper with white spots, gradually caused the leper to lose his or her fingers and toes and eventually claimed his or her life. There was no known cure and it was extremely contagious. Lepers would therefore not only be excluded from the community, but also from worship in the synagogue or in the Temple in Jerusalem. As a result, lepers were totally ostracized from the community, had to scrounge for food, clothing and shelter as best they could and were the poorest of the poor.

When this leper saw Jesus coming, he did something unthinkable in that society. Rather than running *away* from Jesus when he saw him, he ran *towards* him, threw himself down on the ground and begged him, "Sir, if you want to, you can make me clean!" (Matthew 8:2) Jesus then did an astounding thing that must have made the crowd suck in their breath. He reached out and *touched* him! By doing so, he took a great risk. Not only was he breaking social convention, but he was also deliberately exposing himself to becoming infected with this highly contagious and incurable disease.

Then he said and did something even more astounding. He looked at the man with compassion and, where others would have shouted at the man to get away, he said in a kind and compassionate voice, "I do want to. Be clean!" (Matthew 8:3) At once the disease left the man and he was cured! One can't even imagine how he must have felt and how the crowd must have felt.

Jesus then ordered the man to go straight to the priest to be examined according to the law and pronounced officially cured (or 'clean.') He was to offer a sacrifice of thanksgiving and he would then be welcomed back into the community and into the synagogue and the Temple to worship.

This was the greatest demonstration of kindness of all time. It teaches us that a kind person is sensitive to other people's feelings, circumstances and needs and tries to deal with them in a helpful way. It also demonstrates to us that a kind person will often risk her or his own well-being on behalf of the well-being of others. This is the kind of person Jesus consistently was – and the way he wants his followers to be.

For example, Paul sums up Jesus' whole life's goal when he writes, "It is a difficult thing for someone to die for a righteous person. It may even be that someone might dare to die for a good person. But God has shown us how much he loves us - it was while we were still sinners that Christ died for us!" (Romans 5:7-8)

A kind person will be gentle with others. The writer of Proverbs says, "A gentle answer turns away wrath, but a harsh word stirs up anger." (Proverbs 15:1) Paul writes to the Christians at Philippi, "Let your gentleness be evident to all." (Philippians 4:5) He mentions this quality in other letters as one that every Christian should strive to have. (See also Colossians 4:6)

In our culture, aggressiveness and assertiveness are often regarded as virtues while gentleness is considered to be descriptive of wimps, and especially male wimps. But that's not the kind of lifestyle that Jesus taught or modeled. There are times when one must be assertive in order to combat evil, for example, like the time Jesus drove the money changers out of the Temple (See Matthew 21:12-13).

However, when Jesus encountered somebody that was hurting and in need, he dealt with them gently. Therefore, gentleness as an expression of kindness should also be a hallmark of his followers.

A kind person will also be compassionate towards those who are suffering. This was another characteristic that Jesus both taught and modeled. When, for example, he looked at the large crowds listening to him teach (most of which were abjectly poor and powerless), the record says that "He felt compassion for them, because they were weary and worn out, like sheep without a shepherd." (Matthew 9:36)

On another occasion, he and his disciples were headed across Lake Galilee in a boat for a little time away at a deserted place. They had been super busy and Jesus had just learned that his cousin, John the Baptist, had been executed. When the crowds saw where they were headed, they ran around the lake to be there when they landed. By the time they arrived, some 10,000 people (including women and children) had gathered! Rather than being annoyed, like his tired disciples obviously were, the record says that, tired as he was, he had compassion on them and proceeded to spend the whole day teaching them. (See Mark 6:30-34)

A kind person will also be a generous person. The writer of Proverbs states: "Some people spend their money freely and still grow richer. Others are cautious, and yet grow poorer. Be generous, and you will be prosperous. Help others, and you will be helped." (Proverbs 11:24-25) Paul writes to Timothy about how he should encourage Christians to live: "Command them to do good, to be rich in good works, to be generous and ready to share with others. In this way they will store up for themselves a treasure which will be a solid foundation for the future. And then they will be able to win the life which is true life." (1 Timothy 6:18-19)

This was the kind of lifestyle that Jesus lived. For example, after he had finished teaching the huge crowd referred to above, and seeing that they were in the wilderness without any food, despite his disciples' rather sarcastic comments, he proceeded to feed them all! (See Mark 6:35-44)

A kind person will be a friendly and understanding person. The writer of Proverbs says, "Friends always show their love. What are relatives for if not to share trouble?" (Proverbs 17:17) Paul writes to the Ephesians "Be kind and tender-hearted to one another, and forgive one another, as God has forgiven you through Christ." (Ephesians 4:32)

He elaborates on this theme in his letter to the Christians at Colossae: "You must clothe yourselves with compassion, kindness, humility, gentleness, and patience. Be tolerant with one another and forgive one another whenever any of you has a complaint against someone else. You must forgive one another just as the Lord has forgiven you. And to all these qualities add love, which binds all things together in perfect unity." (Colossians 3:12-14)

Again, no one lived a life that more exemplified these characteristics than Jesus Christ. His great mission in life was to befriend the friendless, cheer the downcast, help the needy, heal the sick, bring comfort to the sorrowing, forgive those who lived a sinful life and help the poor and downtrodden. And this is the kind of lifestyle that he calls his followers to live and promises to enable them to live. He knew from experience that showing kindness brings joy, warmth, healing and confidence to others, but it also makes the kind person feel good in heart and useful in life.

Peter, Paul and Gerry

Here are six humorous conversations between Peter, Paul and Gerry, all sending a negative or a positive message about kindness. Read each conversation carefully and answer the questions below.

****

Gerry comes up to Peter and says, "Merry Christmas Pete!" She continues, "During this special time of the year, I think we should put aside our differences and try to be kind." Peter asks, "Why does it only have to be for this time of the year? Why can't it be all year 'round?" To which Gerry replies, "What are you, some kind of fanatic or something?"

****

Peter walks by two girls standing on the sidewalk. One says, 'Well, if it isn't good 'ole Pete!" The other says, "Good ol' wishy-washy Pete!" They both break out laughing, "HA HA HA HA!" Peter keeps walking, a hurt look on his face. Gerry comes along and says, "Hi Pete...Is that your head, or are you hiding behind a balloon?"

As he walks on she too laughs hysterically, "HA HA HA HA HA HA!" while Peter closes his eyes and shakes his head. He then walks home and turns on his TV only to hear a commentator say, "And what in all this world is a more delightful sound than the wonderful laughter of little children?" He gets up and angrily boots the TV across the room.

****

Gerry walks up to her dog Sparky's doghouse. Sparky is lying flat on his back along the tip of the roof. She says, "I don't understand you! You lead such a useless life!! You don't contribute anything! You…" In mid-sentence, Sparky leans over backwards and gives her a kiss on the nose. He resumes his perch and thinks, "A kiss on the nose does much toward turning aside anger."

****

It's New Year's Eve and Gerry is talking to Peter. "Pete, I think you should resolve to be perfect next year." Peter responds, "Perfect? You've got to be kidding! *Nobody's* perfect! What do you expect of me?" Gerry replies, "I think you *can* be if you really try." Peter responds with his hand in the air and a determined look on his face, "Okay, Gerry. If you have that much faith in me, I'll really try! I here and now resolve to be perfect during the coming year!" Gerry screeches with laughter, "YOU? PERFECT?! HA HA HA HA!" Peter looks pained.

****

Peter, all bundled up for the winter, is walking on ice. Suddenly his feet go out from under him and he falls backwards on the ice with a great WHUMP! He looks dazed, tries to get up and exclaims, "I've got so many clothes on, I can't move! I CAN'T GET UP!" He tries again, but in vain, and then says, "It's no use…I'm doomed…I'll never get home…I'll have to lay here until I freeze to death…" Gerry's dog Sparky trots by, sees his predicament, puts his head down and proceeds to shove Peter across the ice towards home while two girls look on with questioning looks on their faces. Peter says to himself, "This is the most humiliating thing that's ever happened to me!"

****

Paul, who loves to listen to classical music, is lying face down on the ground with a frustrated and gloomy look on his face. Gerry is laughing, "HA HA HA HA HA HA! That's the funniest thing I've ever heard! HA HA HA HA HA HA HA!" Paul gets up and begins to walk away with a totally dejected look on his face. Gerry continues, "All year long he waits for Bach's birthday, and then when it finally comes, he *forgets* it! HA HA HA HA HA!" Paul grabs a tree and bangs his head on it.

****

1. In your opinion, which conversation best illustrates the concept of kindness and why?

2. Which best illustrates the opposite of the concept of kindness and why?

3. Which character in these conversations do you most identify with and why?

4. According to these conversations, when people are unkind to others, what feelings does this kind of behavior provoke?

5. Conversely, when people are kind to others, what feelings does this kind of behavior provoke?

What Does This Tell You About Yourself?

1. Did you have an easy time making your choices? Explain.

2. Who is the kindest person you have ever met? Why did you choose that person?

3. Would you describe yourself as a kind person most of the time? Explain.

4. "Thinking about being a kind person makes me want to…………………..

Chapter Eight

THE LAST SHALL BE FIRST

> **Read All About It!**
>
> Read about a man who had to HUMBLE himself in order to get well in 2 Kings 5:1-116.

From Peasant to Pope to Peasant Pope

On September 28, 1978, a sudden heart attack ended the brief reign of Pope John Paul I. Just five weeks before, one of the shortest conclaves in the history of the Roman Catholic Church had elected the relatively unknown 65 year-old Albino Luciani, Patriarch of Venice, as the 263rd Pope. His warm smile and humble simplicity quickly won the hearts of millions. Then, almost as quickly, John Paul was dead!

His papacy lasted only 34 days. He gave no major speeches, wrote no encyclicals and made no important appointments. But in the short month that he reigned as Pope John Paul I, he demonstrated to the whole world that the head of the Roman Catholic Church was not meant to be a prince, but a pastor. He brought simple humble gifts to the papacy - a ready smile, a tendency to laugh and joke and a hug for almost everyone he met. He didn't have enough time to deal with substantial matters, but John Paul's compelling personal style gave the Roman Catholic Church a brief time of renewed hope and promise.

From the beginning, John Paul used his Sunday sermons and Wednesday public audiences to talk to his flock like a father and a friend. The first thing he did was to drop the impersonal papal 'we.' Appearing on the balcony after his election, he said to the vast throng in St. Peter's Square below, "Yesterday morning, I came to the Sistine Chapel to vote quietly." The crowd burst into appreciative cheers. His manner recalled the warmth and simplicity of the papacy of the much-loved John XXIII. His sudden death elicited genuine grief around the world.

Just days before he was chosen as the new Pope, an NBC newsman in Rome telephoned him to ask him for some biographical information. With characteristic humility, Luciani said: "There's a Class A list of candidates, a Class B list of candidates, and a Class C list of candidates. I'm surely on the Class C list." His fellow Cardinals obviously disagreed.

Later, when speaking to a crowd in St. Peter's Square, the new Pope referred to his two predecessors. "I don't have the wisdom of Pope John or the preparation and culture of Pope Paul," he said, "but I am in their place. I hope you will help me with your prayers."

The new Pope was born and raised in the village of Canale d'Agordo in the Dolomite Alps. When news of his election reached his fellow townspeople, they were surprised and held a quiet celebration. One local priest, who was one of Luciani's oldest friends, remarked, "The people are happy, but in the style of mountain people, their joy is inner rather than outer. The new Pope is also this way." John Paul would have agreed.

He once called himself "The little man accustomed to little things and to silence." But he accepted his new role with the same obedience, the same smile and the same humility that had characterized the rest of his career.

John Paul's friends described him as an easygoing man with a gentle sense of humor and a talent for conciliation. He insisted on a simple coronation that was in accord with his own humble origins, his simple tastes and his deeply felt concern for the poor. The new Pope was a pastor above all else.

Luciani's father had been a glass-worker. He had provided for his family in a tiny shack around a wood burning stove. After World War I, the family was so poor that the children wore wooden clogs and ate grass and nettles. His younger brother, Eduardo, remembered, "Once Albino brought me a piece of white bread that someone had given him. Neither of us had seen white bread before, but Albino gave it to me. I still remember the taste."

Luciani became a professor of dogmatic theology at the Belluno Seminary in the 1940s. There, he taught the faith in terms that were as simple as possible so the illiterate mountain people could understand it. He published a book called *Catechism Crumbs*, which by 1978 was already in its seventh printing. One of the first things he did as the Patriarch of Venice was to ask local parishes to sell their jewels and give the money to those in need. Luciani used to wade through big snowdrifts to pay his regular pastoral calls. He would greet parishioners with a casual "Come va?!" or "How's it going?"
Luciani lived a Spartan life in Venice. A friend from his native village once visited him there. He brought a whole hamper of locally grown food, but Luciani only accepted two walnuts. "That's enough for my supper," he said.

John Paul was a Pope who through his pastoral gestures built a bridge between himself and the common people he loved. At the time of Luciani's death, Cardinal Francois Marty of Paris said, "The Pope had a message to give our world. He gave us the message. He gave us the smile of God. In the grayness of these days, this smile will remain like a beam of light. Perhaps it was this message of universal love which exhausted him. That was enough. His work was accomplished."

And then, in 2013, it happened all over again! Upon the resignation of Pope Benedict XVI, Jorge Mario Bergoglio became the first Pope to be elected from Latin America. Like Pope John Paul, throughout his public life, Pope Francis had been noted for his humility, his emphasis on God's mercy and his concern for the poor. He chose the name Francis after the famous St. Francis of Assisi who turned his back on his family wealth and devoted his life to serving the poor.

Born of Italian immigrant parents in Buenos Aires, Argentina in 1936, Pope Francis worked briefly as a chemical technologist and nightclub bouncer before feeling called to the priesthood and beginning seminary studies. He was ordained a Catholic priest in 1969 and from 1973 to 1979 was Argentina's provincial superior of the Society of Jesus.

Bergoglio became the Archbishop of Buenos Aires in 1998 and worked hard to increase the Church's presence in the slums of Buenos Aires to the point where he was dubbed 'the Slum Bishop.' Under his leadership, the number of priests assigned to work in the slums doubled. He made it his custom to celebrate the Holy Thursday ritual of washing of feet in places such as jails, hospitals, retirement homes or slums.

Bishop Bergoglio was made a Cardinal in 2001 by Pope John Paul II. He became known for his persona of humility and for his commitment to social justice. His simple lifestyle contributed to his reputation for humility. He chose to live in a small apartment, rather than in the elegant bishop's residence in the suburb of Olivos. He took public transportation and cooked his own meals.

Since his election as Pope, Francis has taken a more humble and informal approach to the papacy than his predecessors. For example, he chose to reside in a simple church guest house rather than in the lavish papal apartments. He insists on carrying his own luggage and is known for favoring simpler vestments - refusing to don the traditional papal cape upon his election, choosing silver instead of gold for his papal ring, and keeping the same cross he had as a Cardinal.

He champions the cause of the poor and urges the church to be more open and welcoming, particularly to those who are struggling and to minorities. As such, he has endeared himself to the faithful, opened the doors of the Roman Catholic Church to welcome those who were shunned and become a world-renowned figure.

All the while, he continues to practice deeds of humility and service to the poorest of the poor, those in prison, orphans and widows and the like. Like Pope John Paul I before him, he has become an authentic witness to Jesus' teaching that "The first will be last and the last will be first." (Matthew 20:16)

An Exercise in Humility

1. Who are three other prominent people you know about who strike you as being symbols of humility? Explain your choices.

2. Some wag once said, "Did you hear about the guy who wrote a book entitled *Humility...and How I Attained It*?" What point was he making?

3. How would you rate yourself in the humility department in comparison to Popes John Paul I and Francis and the three people you selected in question 1?

The Lifestyle of Jesus

When it came to the subject of humility, Jesus called on his followers to aim high by kneeling low. "Those who make themselves great in the sight of people now will be humbled in the Kingdom of God, but those who are humble in the sight of God and people now, will be made great in the Kingdom of God." (Luke 14:11) Or again, "Whoever wants to be first must place himself last and be the servant of all." (Mark 9:35)

Jesus once told a story about two men who went to the Temple to pray. One was a tax collector (who belonged to a group of rogues who worked for the Roman occupiers and could charge whatever they could squeeze out of people), and the other was a Pharisee (who belonged to a group of people who thought they could win God's favor through their own efforts to do what was right and who looked down on those who couldn't).

The Pharisee's prayer was first of all filled with a catalogue of all the bad things that he wasn't: he wasn't greedy; he wasn't a crook; he wasn't an adulterer (and one could probably add quite a few other items to his laundry list). Then he went on to list all the good things he had done: he had fasted twice a week and he had given a tenth of his income to God (and again, one could probably add a good number of items to that list as well). Finally, he boosted his own position by comparing himself favorably with those who, in his eyes, weren't up to snuff. He hadn't done bad things "like everybody else" and he was certainly better than "that tax collector over there."

Meanwhile, the tax collector didn't even dare to look up, but stood way off in a corner beating on his chest in contrition and praying, "Lord, have pity on me a sinner!" Jesus concludes the story by surprising his audience (who had been taught that 'good' people can earn their salvation in the sight of God by doing 'good things') by turning the tables upside down. The contrite 'sinner' went home justified, he said, but the self-righteous 'goodie' went away with nothing but the *illusion* that he was justified. (See Luke 18:9-14)

In telling this story, Jesus teaches his followers a number of lessons about pride and humility.

1. Proud people will think they're better than others (in appearance, ability, intelligence, behavior, belief, etc.), while humble people will realize that all people are of equal value before God.

2. Proud people will put down others to build themselves up, while humble people will realize that all people stand in equal need of God's grace and forgiveness.

3. Proud people will call attention to their own abilities and achievements, while humble people will realize that all abilities are gifts; that all achievements are merely the fulfillment of responsibility; and that all people have abilities of one kind or another.

4. Proud people will not admit their errors/mistakes/sins, while humble people will contritely confess them.

5. Proud people will want to be first, be served and be praised (often at the expense of others), while humble people will concentrate on accepting, encouraging and serving others in order to help them meet their needs and develop their potential.

On another occasion, Jesus had to more or less hit his own disciples over the head to make these points when they were arguing about which one of them was the greatest!

> "Jesus asked his disciples, 'What were you arguing about on the road?' But they would not answer him, because on the road they had been arguing among themselves about who was the greatest. Jesus sat down, called the twelve disciples, and said to them, 'Whoever wants to be first must place himself last of all and be the servant of all.' Then he took a child and had him stand in front of them. He put his arms around him and said to them, 'Whoever welcomes in my name one of these children, welcomes me; and whoever welcomes me, welcomes not only me but also the one who sent me.'" (Mark 9:33-37)

Why did he place a young child in front of them and say what he did about young children? Because young children had no status in society. They had no power, no wealth and no advanced education or experience. They were simply to be obedient to their parents and others who had authority over them. And they were innocent in that they had not yet completely learned how to advance themselves at the expense of others or perfected their skills of deception. In fact, they would even blurt out things they 'weren't supposed to tell' when it came to family secrets or whatever.

Shortly after this incident, Jesus clearly spelled it out loud and clear. James and John came to him privately and asked him to do them a favor.

> "When you sit on your throne in your glorious Kingdom, we want you to let us sit with you, one at your right and one at your left." When the other

The Last Shall Be First

> disciples heard about it, they became angry. So Jesus called them all together and said, "You know that those who are considered rulers of the heathen have power over them, and the leaders have complete authority. This, however, is not the way it is among you. If one of you wants to be great, you must be the servant of the rest; and if one of you wants to be first, you must be the slave of all. For even the Son of Man did not come to be served; he came to serve and to give his life to redeem many people." (Mark 10:35-45)

And then he demonstrated what he had taught them during their last supper together when, in place of the usual slave, he astounded them by getting down on his knees and washing their dirty smelly sandaled feet! When he had finished, he said,

> "Do you understand what I have just done to you?...
> You call me Teacher and Lord, and it is right that you do so, because that is what I am. I, your Lord and Teacher, have just washed your feet. You, then, should wash one another's feet. I have set an example for you, so that you will do just what I have done for you. I am telling you the truth: no slaves are greater than their master, and no messengers are greater than the one who sent them. Now that you know this truth, how happy you will be if you put it into practice!" (John 13:12-17)

What Do *You* Think?

1. Read through each of the following statements and explain in your own words what you think each is saying. If you want more background information on the circumstances surrounding these statements, look up the references given and read the section in which each statement appears.

2. Then rank these statements in the order in which in your opinion they best teach something vital about humility.

3. Finally, explain why you chose what you did as your first choice and your last choice.

   ❖ "It is better to be humble and stay poor than to be one of the arrogant and get a share of their loot." (Proverbs.16:19)

   ❖ "God resists the proud, but gives grace to the humble." (James 4:6)

   ❖ "The greatest in the Kingdom of heaven is the one who humbles himself and becomes like a child." (Matthew 18:4)

   ❖ "'You must be humble before you can ever receive honors." (Proverbs 15:33)

   ❖ "Everyone who makes himself great will be humbled, and everyone who humbles himself will be made great." (Luke 14:11)

   ❖ "Arrogance will bring your downfall, but if you are humble, you will be respected." (Proverbs 29:23)

   ❖ "A day is coming when human pride will be ended and human arrogance destroyed. On that day the Lord Almighty will humble everyone who is powerful, everyone who is proud and conceited." (Isaiah 2:11-12)

   ❖ "Have reverence for the Lord, be humble, and you will get riches, honor and a long life." (Proverbs 22:4)

- ❖ "The attitude you should have is the one that Christ Jesus had...He was humble and walked the path of obedience all the way to death." (Philippians 2:5,8)

- ❖ "Humble yourselves, then, under God's mighty hand, so that he will lift you up in his own good time." (I Peter 5:6)

What Does This Tell You About Yourself?

1. "I think I am/am not a very humble person because ....

2. "I think people who are humble will ....

3. "The most humble person I have ever met was _____ because s/he ....

4. "Some things I need to work on in my life in this area are ....

Chapter Nine

WHO CARES!?

> **Read All About It!**
>
> Read about expressing CONCERN through giving in 1 Corinthians 9:6-15.

A Letter Home

February 2, 2001

"Dear Mom,

Thanks for your welcome letter which I received yesterday. You're right. It's been a year now since I left San Francisco for Hong Kong, and it seems as though the time has just flown by. It's the end of the semester and I've just finished grading final exam papers. I'm glad *that* job is over with and that the summer break is almost here. I think I would actually enjoy grading essay papers if there weren't so many to do at once. My senior high kids write interesting things about their lives at home and in this great city that give me a much deeper insight into their lives and into the realities of life in Hong Kong.

"It's strange. When I first arrived, I was just like most other tourists. I noticed the forests of impressive buildings, enjoyed the beautiful beaches, sampled lots of the great food and went on shopping sprees. I remember passing by some of the squatter areas, noticing how crowded some places were, seeing some beggars on the streets, etc, but that all seemed quite far away from me. As I wrote to you before, I was having a ball looking at the beautiful side of Hong Kong's 'postcard' and ignoring the other side - the ugly side that I didn't want to see and didn't know much about.

"My high school seniors changed all that. As I got to know them over the year and began to counsel them when they came to me with their problems, I began to realize that my stay here was going to involve a lot more than simply teaching English and having a ball. I was going to have to give a lot more of myself to these kids and to this place than I had counted on.

"You remember David Chan that I wrote to you about? Since that letter, I've discovered that he lives in the New Territories an hour and a half bus ride from the school. That means that he loses three hours of study time every day because the bus is too bouncy for him to be able to do any reading. His father died five years ago. His mother works every day and expects him, as the eldest son, to look after the three smaller kids when he gets home, and to help with the cooking and the housework. On Saturdays, he works all morning washing dishes for a little local restaurant to earn a little extra money for the family. Needless to say, he's under increasing pressure at school, and his work isn't up to standard. Well, he came into my office a few days ago and poured out his heart to me.

"I was in a terrible rush, but I made myself give him the time he needed. I couldn't do much more for him then to listen and make a few practical suggestions, but he was visibly moved that somebody cared. You just can't imagine how many kids there are in similar desperate circumstances here.

"Tonight I go to a meeting of the Society for the Blind. Believe it or not, I'm involved in a program to learn how to read Braille so I can help translate more books into Braille for the considerable number of blind people here. You even see some of them begging on the streets. I hope the work that I and others are doing will help to increase the opportunities for blind people here to live a normal and decent life.

"Next Wednesday afternoon, I'll supervise the study hall and tutorial program our church has begun for secondary school kids in the area. Many of these kids live in crowded resettlement estates where there's lots of noise and little privacy for study Most of their parents can't afford to hire tutors to help these kids with their school work so they'll have a more equal chance to vie with kids of well-to-do parents for the university seats here.

"These and similar activities really keep me busy. I'm afraid I won't have as much time for partying and lazing on the beach as I used to. In fact, now that I think about it, that's about all I used to do at home, other than attend classes! Mom, you may not believe it, but I think coming to Hong Kong has helped me to realize how self-centered I've been. I think I'm finally beginning to realize that life can be much more meaningful when you begin to be concerned about other people's needs and do something about them.

"Of course, I still have some fun here too! Well, I must close for now. Hope all's well at home. Take care of yourself and give my love to Dad…..and tell him to write sometime!

Love, Pat

P.S. I saw this on a poster the other day.

'I WONDERED WHY SOMEBODY DIDN'T DO SOMETHING. THEN I REALIZED THAT *I WAS THAT SOMEBODY!'"

****

If you were writing a letter to your Mother, what efforts to be of help to people in need could you write about?

The Lifestyle of Jesus

Jesus taught us a great deal about being concerned about other people's needs and demonstrated what that means in practical terms. For example, as we've seen, he once provided food for some ten thousand people when they were stuck out in the wilderness with no restaurant or grocery nearby. But there's more to that story.

The disciples were obviously on a different wave length than Jesus on that occasion. They'd just returned from a strenuous mission and were looking forward to a little 'R & R.' When they saw the huge crowd that had beat them to the other side of the lake and knew that Jesus was not going to take a detour to avoid it, they must have given a big sigh of disappointment. That disappointment grew into impatience when Jesus went on to use up the rest of the day teaching the people.

Finally, they interrupted Jesus to remind him of the lateness of the hour and asked him to send the people away so they could go home and get some food (and so that they would be rid of the crowd and could still get some time alone to rest and relax!). Where Jesus looked at the crowd as a great big opportunity, they looked at that same crowd as a great big problem. They still had a lot to learn about the fact that concern for others means to notice other people's needs and to do something about them; to see other people's difficulties as opportunities for ministry not as problems to be ignored or avoided.

And where did the food that Jesus blessed and multiplied to feed that crowd come from? In John's account of this incident, he tells us that when Jesus instructed the disciples to see what food they could find, they came back with five rolls and two fish that they had scrounged from a boy in the crowd. (See John 6:1-15) Why did the boy give up his lunch? He could have said, "If the rest of these people were too stupid to bring food with them, why should I give them mine?" But he apparently gladly gave his lunch to Jesus because he trusted him to do the right thing with it. He must have been astounded to see what he *did* do with it! And he, and the disciples, learned that day that concern means to share what we have with those in need no matter how great the need or how small our resources. (See Matthew 14:13-21; Luke 9:10-17)

On another occasion, in response to the question, "Who is my neighbor?" Jesus told a story about a Jew being attacked by robbers, beaten up and left on the road half dead. Obviously, if the man is going to survive, he's going to need somebody to help him. A Levite (who was responsible to help keep things running smoothly at the Temple) comes along. Surely, the listening crowd thinks, *he* will help the man. But, surprisingly, he crosses over to the other side of the road to *avoid* him and continues on his way.

Then a priest comes along. Again, the crowd thinks that, being a religious leader, he will *certainly* take pity on the man and help him. And he does pause to go over and look at him, but then, surprisingly, also goes on his way doing nothing to help. (Was he afraid of getting his beautiful robes soiled?)

Finally, a Samaritan comes along. The crowd has no expectations here. Since the Jews despised the Samaritans, they assume that he will surely pay no attention to the wounded Jew. But surprise, surprise! He not only helps the man by pouring oil on his wounds and bandaging them up, but by picking him up, putting him on his donkey and taking him to an inn. And then, almost unbelievably, he asks the inn keeper to put him up and take care of him until he is well again – and he will pay him whatever it costs! (See Luke 10:25-37)

What was Jesus trying to teach the crowd (and us) by telling this story? First, that *every* person (even those who despise me or whom I despise) is my neighbor! And therefore every person's need should be my concern. Second, that it costs to be concerned. It cost the Samaritan time, energy, money and the risk of also being attacked by those same robbers. And what was his wife going to say when he got home with his clothes full of blood and tried to explain to her why he had spent their hard earned money on a Jew!? Third, that the more I know about the meaning of loving concern for others, the more responsible I am to demonstrate that concern and to do something concrete about it. The Levite and the Priest were long on theory when it came to their religion, but obviously short on practice.

On still another occasion, Jesus talked about inviting people over for dinner. "When you give a lunch or a dinner, do not invite your friends or your brothers or your relatives or your rich neighbors - for they will invite you back, and in this way you will be paid for what you did. When you give a feast, invite the poor, the crippled, the lame, and the blind; and you will be blessed, because they are not able to pay you back. God will repay you on the day the good people rise from death." (Luke 14:12-14)

He of course didn't mean that people should never invite their friends, neighbors or relatives over for dinner, but that they shouldn't neglect to invite the poor, the stranger, the lonely, the homeless and the handicapped as well. The main point he was making was to point out that to be concerned for others means that we'll think in terms of self-giving rather than in terms of self-getting.

Somebody will inevitably remark, "If I did that with every stranger and needy person I met or knew about, I'd be broke in a month!" Jesus often used hyperbole to get people's attention, which is the case here. He's simply pointing out that we too often *only* want to be with people we know, who think like us, whom we enjoy, who don't have big problems and who can reciprocate - and not with anybody else.

Perhaps his yardstick on this subject would be - be concerned with meeting the needs of others up to the point where you yourself would become a concern for others. This is what he meant when he reiterated the great principle on this subject from the Old Testament: "Love your neighbor as yourself." (Leviticus 19:18) To love our neighbor is not to abandon our concern for self, but to put our concern for our neighbors on a par with our concern for ourselves.

Jesus summed up his teaching about what being concerned for others is all about in what has become known as 'The Golden Rule' - "Do for others what you want them to do for you: this is the meaning of the Law of Moses and of the teachings of the prophets." (Matthew 7:12)

An Art Contest

Imagine that you're a judge in an art contest. You're to choose the 'Concern Piece of the Year' from the group of drawings below.

1. Rank them in the order of your preference.

2. Explain why you chose what you did for your first and last choices.

3. Think up a caption for each drawing that describes what you think it says about 'concern,' with each caption beginning, "Concern is ……."

4. Which drawing can you best imagine yourself being 'in'? Why?

Who Cares?   Page |89

What Does This Tell You About Yourself?

1. "I had a hard/easy time making my choice because ………

2. "I could/couldn't easily fit into most of these drawings because ……….

3. "I find it easy/hard to be concerned about other people's needs because ………

4. "I feel this process has helped me to ………..

Chapter Ten

BE FORGIVING AND ENJOY LIVING

> **Read All About It!**
>
> Read about a man who FORGAVE his killers
> while being killed in Acts 7:51-60.

A Night at the Movies

I settled down in my seat and munched on a bag of popcorn while the commercials and the previews flashed by on the screen. Finally the feature appeared, scrawled out in big letters across the screen – 'THE GAMBLER.'

"The story began in the apartment of a young couple with two small children. They were laughing and having a good time playing together. Before long, the children were put to bed and Adam and his pretty wife Jean relaxed on the couch, reading the newspaper and listening to music on their IPod. The music was romantic, and before long, Adam had his arm around Jean who snuggled up against him with her feet tucked up on the couch.

"They began to reminisce about how they had first met eight years before. While they were talking, flashbacks of their romance and early years together appeared on the screen. Before long, they got up, turned out the light and went into the bedroom.

"The next morning, Adam kissed Jean and the children goodbye and drove off to his job at the bank. While driving, he thought back to the day he'd first applied for a job as a lowly teller and of how he'd rapidly risen through the ranks until today he had almost everything that a young family man dreams about. Again, the camera followed his thoughts by flashing scenes of the past on the screen.

"Adam put in his usual busy day at the bank. That afternoon, one of his customers asked if he'd like to go to the Casino that night and have a little fun. He agreed and called Jean to tell her that he wouldn't be coming home until later in the evening.

"After a great meal at the Casino, Adam sat down with his friend at the Poker Table and looked in wonder at the sights in the fancy Casino. He'd been to the races now and then, but it was small potatoes compared to this! He'd also begun to buy a few Lottery tickets at the gas station a few times a month after he'd started earning more money at the bank. Sometimes he'd won a few bucks, and sometimes he hadn't.

"The round began, and Adam picked up his hand. As the evening wore on, his friend began to bet larger and larger sums of money. The excitement of winning and losing became contagious and Adam followed suit. When they finally quit, he went home happy with more money in his pocket than he'd come with!

"The plot then began to thicken. Adam began to go to the Casino with his friend once or twice a month and stop by the gas station once a week. The more he went, the more his 'fever' increased until before long, he was going to the

Casino once a week and to the gas station every few days. Some weeks he would win and some weeks he would lose.

"Jean began to be concerned about the time and money that Adam was spending on gambling. They began to have arguments about it, and their relationship became more and more tense. Jean worried out loud that he would lose too much money and get them into financial trouble. Adam laughed or got angry in turn and tried to convince her that he knew what he was doing and that he'd win more than he would lose. But it remained a festering sore between them.

"Then the inevitable happened. Adam began to bet larger sums to increase the excitement - and he began to lose. The more he lost, the more he bet in a desperate bid to wipe out his losses with a lucky 'big win.' He had long age begun to secretly tap into the family savings. Now he began to secretly barrow money. The cycle got worse, but he'd now become a gambling addict and couldn't find the strength to break the habit.

"Jean was a smart woman. She wasn't fooled by all of Adam's attempted cover-ups. Their relationship continued to deteriorate. Their arguments became fierce. She'd tearfully beg him to stop before he lost his job and ruined their future. Sometimes he'd listen, be sorry and promise to quit - and she'd forgive him. But he couldn't bring himself to keep his promises. Once she threatened to divorce him and this shocked them both as they loved each other deeply. For awhile after that he quit, but then the old fever got the better of him and he went back to the Casino and the gas station again.

"One day he went to work as usual, but he left the bank that day without a job! His supervisor had warned him a number of times that his gambling habits were interfering with his work.

His worry over his heavy debts had increasingly taken his mind off his business, and his performance had slumped. His supervisor felt badly because Adam had had such a good record at the bank before, but he now had no choice but to fire him.

"Adam didn't go home. He walked through the streets in a daze and sat down on a park bench with his head in his hands. How could he face Jean? The shock of losing his job jarred him to his senses. He vowed that HE WOULD QUIT ONCE AND FOR ALL!! He would never again place another bet! He'd start again at the bottom and rebuild what they'd had before! He'd go home and plead with Jean to forgive him one more time. He would concentrate on rebuilding their loving relationship even though the circumstances would be difficult.

"With a new sense of determination, he got up got into his car and eventually arrived at their house. Jean met him at the door............." and suddenly everything went black! All the lights in the theater were off! The emergency lights came on and a man announced that he was very sorry, but that there had been a power outage in the area. There would be no electricity for at least two more hours.

"I got up from my seat, along with the rest of the crowd, and we all grumbled as we left the theater. How would the story end? We would now have no chance to find out."

****

How do *you* think the story ended? What would *you* have done if you had been Jean, and why?

The Lifestyle of Jesus

Once, Jesus' disciple Peter asked him, "Lord, if my brother keeps on sinning against me, how many times do I have to forgive him? Seven times?" (Matthew 18:21) Why seven? The Jewish Rabbis taught that a person should forgive another person three times. By more than doubling that, Peter thought he would be commended by Jesus. Instead, Jesus astounded him by saying, "No, not seven times, but seventy times seven." (Matthew 18:22) In other words, he was to forgive without limit! Then Jesus told a story to illustrate his point.

> "Once there was a king who decided to check on his servants' accounts. He had just begun to do so when one of them was brought in who owed him millions of dollars. The servant did not have enough to pay his debt, so the king ordered him to be sold as a slave, with his wife and his children and all that he had, in order to pay the debt. The servant fell on his knees before the king. 'Be patient with me,' he begged, 'and I will pay you everything!' The king felt sorry for him, so he forgave him the debt and let him go.
>
> "Then the man went out and met one of his fellow servants who owed him a few dollars. He grabbed him and started choking him. 'Pay back what you owe me!' he said. His fellow servant fell down and begged him, 'Be patient with me, and I will pay you back!' But he refused; instead, he had him thrown into jail until he should pay the debt.
>
> "When the other servants saw what had happened, they were very upset and went to the king and told him everything. So he called the servant in. 'You worthless slave!' he said. 'I forgave you the whole amount you owed me, just because you asked me to. You should have had mercy on your fellow servant, just as I had mercy on you.' The king was very angry, and he sent the servant to jail to be punished until he should pay back the whole amount."

"And Jesus concluded, 'That is how my Father in heaven will treat every one of you unless you forgive your brother from your heart.'" (Matthew 18:21-35)

A number of principles about forgiveness can be drawn from this story.

- ❖ If we're unwilling to forgive others, we don't deserve forgiveness ourselves.

- ❖ We should be willing to forgive others as often as they sincerely ask us to.

- ❖ Forgiveness must be "from the heart" or it's worthless.

- ❖ To be forgiven, a person must be sincerely sorry and willing to change.

- ❖ We all owe an unpayable moral debt to God since we've fallen short of the potential he's given us. He stands ready to forgive us if we own up to our shortcomings and sincerely want to change what needs to be changed in our lives.

- ❖ A person can't earn or deserve forgiveness; s/he can only humbly receive it.

- ❖ If we're willing to forgive others, it proves that we've understood the real meaning of forgiveness as it applies to us.

One of the greatest stories that Jesus ever told was a story about a wealthy father and his two sons. The younger son (totally against the custom of that culture) brashly asks his father for his share of the inheritance and promptly leaves home (again, an unheard of act). He goes to a far country and wastes his entire inheritance on wine, women and song. At his wits end and out of sheer desperation, he finally gets a job as a pig herder (yet again, an unheard of occupation for a Jew) and is reduced to eating even less than what the pigs eat!

At last, he comes to his senses and owns up to how foolish and wrong he's been. He makes it back to his father's house half starving and in rags. He confesses to his father that he's not only grievously sinned against him, but also against his heavenly father. He begs for forgiveness, says that he's no longer worthy to be called his son and asks if he can simply live and work at home as a hired servant.

His father, overjoyed that his wayward son has returned, embraces him and not only receives him back as a son, but gives him new clothes and a ring and throws a big welcome home party! But, the older son, rather than forgiving his brother as his father has, is angry. He refuses to come to the party and tells his father that he's worked for him like a slave for many years and never disobeyed his orders. He accuses his father of never having given him anything, not even a goat so he could have a party with his friends.

The father replies, "My son, you're always here with me, and everything I have is yours. But we had to celebrate and be happy, because your brother was dead, but now he's alive; he was lost, but now he's been found." (See Luke 15:11-32)

What can we learn from *this* story?

- ❖ Nobody could have sunk lower than the younger son, but in the end, there's no offense that's unforgiveable. Jesus even forgave the thief on the cross at the last minute. (See Luke 23:39-43)

- ❖ To experience forgiveness, like the younger son, we must recognize that we've done wrong and repent (change direction). We must return to those we've wronged, confess our wrong doing and ask God and them for forgiveness.

- ❖ In one way or another, we too are like the younger son. God made us able to live a complete and meaningful life in fellowship with him. We've too often misused much of what he gave us. As a result, our lives are less meaningful and we sometimes feel far away from God. However, he always stands ready to forgive us and welcome us back 'home' so that we can again begin to live as he intended.

- ❖ Like the older brother, people who feel that they don't need forgiveness have failed to look hard enough at their own attitudes and actions. In the end, *everybody* needs forgiveness. Paul writes: "For *all* have sinned and fallen short of the glory of God." (Romans 3:23)

- ❖ Some of the reasons why people like the older brother won't forgive others are jealousy, pride, hatred, and revenge.

- ❖ Forgiveness brings the joy of reconciliation between us and others and between God and us. Paul writes:

"But God has shown us how much he loves us - it was while we were still sinners that Christ died for us! By his blood we are now put right with God; how much more, then, will we be saved by him from God's anger! We were God's enemies, but he made us his friends through the death of his Son. Now that we are God's friends, how much more will we be saved by Christ's life! But that is not all; we rejoice because of what God has done through our Lord Jesus Christ, who has now made us God's friends." (Romans 5:8-11)

Teaching is one thing, *doing* is another. Jesus not only left us with lofty words, but with an unbelievable example. At the end of his life on earth, he suffered horribly. From his own disciples he suffered betrayal, denial and desertion. From the Jews he suffered insults, mockery, injustice and beating. From the Romans he suffered injustice, whipping, thorns, mockery, spitting, beating and death by slow torture. From one of the bandits who were crucified with him, he suffered insults. And yet, with almost his last breath he prayed, "Forgive them, Father! They don't know what they are doing." (See Matthew 26:56, 65-68; 27:27-31, 35-44; Luke 23:32-34)

Jesus taught that we should love and be willing to forgive even our worst enemies. (See Matthew 5:42-48) Throughout his life, and especially during his agonizing death, he demonstrated by his example that a *willingness* to forgive is an act of love that reaches out to those who offend or persecute or sin against us even if they don't yet admit their need for forgiveness.

What Do *You* Think?

Read through each of the following statements and rephrase in your own words what you think each statement is saying. Then chose the three statements that mean the most to you and explain why you chose them.

- "If we confess our sins to God, he will keep his promise and do what is right: he will forgive us our sins and purify us from all our wrong-doing." (1 John 1:9)

- "If you forgive others the wrongs they have done to you, your Father in heaven will also forgive you. But if you do not forgive others, then your Father will not forgive the wrongs you have done." (Matthew 6:14-15)

- "Happy are those whose sins are forgiven, whose wrongs are pardoned." (Psalm 32:1)

- "Lord, if my brother keeps on sinning against me, how many times do I have to forgive him? Seven times?" "No, not seven times," answered Jesus, "but seventy times seven." (Matthew 18:21-22)

- "Be kind and tender-hearted to one another, and forgive one another, as God has forgiven you through Christ." (Ephesians 4:32)

- "Praise the Lord, my soul, and do not forget how kind he is. He forgives all my sins …. As far as the east is from the west, so far does he remove our sins from us." (Psalm 103: 2-3, 12)

- "It is through Jesus that the message about forgiveness of sins is preached to you; and that everyone who believes in him is set free from all the sins from which the Law of Moses could not set you free." (Acts 13:38-39)

- ❖ "I will get up and go to my father and say, 'Father, I have sinned against God and against you.' .... He was still a long way from home when his father saw him; his heart was filled with pity, and he ran, threw his arms around his son, and kissed him." (Luke 15:18-20)

- ❖ "By the death of Christ we are set free, that is, our sins are forgiven." (Ephesians 1:7)

- ❖ "Jacob went ahead of them and bowed down to the ground seven times as he approached his brother. But Esau ran to meet him and kissed him. They were both crying." (Genesis 33:3-4)

- ❖ "Then Joseph said to them, 'Please come closer.' They did, and he said, 'I am your brother Joseph, whom you sold into Egypt. Now do not be upset or blame yourselves because you sold me here. It was really God who sent me ahead of you to save people's lives." (Genesis 45:4-5)

- ❖ "Joseph threw his arms around his brother Benjamin and began to cry; Benjamin also cried as he hugged him. Then, still weeping, he embraced each of his brothers and kissed them. After that, his brothers began to talk with him." (Genesis 45: 14-15)

What Does This Tell You About Yourself?

1. "As I look back over my life, the three people who have had to forgive me most often are ....

2. "The three people I've had to forgive most often are ....

3. "There are some things I've still not forgiven others for or been forgiven by others. When thinking about those things, I would like to ....…...

4. "I feel that to confess my sins to God and ask for his forgiveness is ....

Chapter Eleven

ARE YOU A CONSTRUCTIVE PERSON?

> **Read All About It!**
>
> Read how a CONSTRUCTIVE person treats others in James 2:1-9.

Retribution or Reformation?

Members of the Rotary, it gives me great pleasure to take this opportunity to address you on the urgent question of prison reform.

"At this moment, there are thousands of men and women sitting in jails in America - people who are lonely, frustrated and angry; angry at themselves and many of them angry at society. (I don't need to remind you how many people like this there are throughout the world!) The fact that this many people are behind bars (and their number continues to grow) itself demands that we continually ask ourselves as a society why we've placed them there, what we're doing with or to them and what effect this is having upon them.

"Most people would be quick to say that we've placed people in jail because they're guilty of some unacceptable anti-social behavior; they've done something wrong. They would also be quick to point out that they're there in order to be punished, and that the severity of their punishment is determined by the gravity of their crime. However, many people would be less sure about what effect this experience is having upon those who sit in our prisons. They really wouldn't know, although the ever increasing costs for law enforcement, trial procedures and the running of prisons gives them some nagging doubts as to the effectiveness of it all.

"And indeed those doubts are justified. The number of those who return to prison after a first offence is way too high. Why should this be so if our system of punishment as retribution and as a deterrent to further crime is valid? Even worse, many who are jailed for minor crimes and are first time offenders become hardened criminals during their stay in prison. Statistics show that they will go on to engage in more serious crime upon leaving their prison cells. A good number of these will have become drug addicts as well. The discouraging fact is that we now have more police and prisoners than ever before, but, after decades of declining violent crime rates, those rates and the number of criminals has once again begun to rise. Why?

"I contend that one reason for this is that by and large, we are putting people in prison for the wrong reasons and treating them with the wrong methods. I maintain that our chief objective in the imprisonment of offenders should not be retribution, but reformation. That is, our aim should not be to inflict social revenge, but to extend social compassion - to help people realize where and why they've gone wrong and how they can change their lives in such a way that they will become assets to our society rather than liabilities. In short, we need to seriously implement what I would call the 'Four Rs' in the way we treat our prisoners: recognition, repentance, restitution and renewal.

"The first step in the reformation of criminals should be to help them to **Recognize** that what they've done has been harmful to themselves and to others. This takes a great deal of empathetic, patient counseling that helps them explore their lives and voluntarily own up to their problem. Criminals are like alcoholics, they will do nothing about their problem until they recognize that they have one and understand something about *why* they have one.

"The second step should be to give criminals an opportunity to **Repent** of their misdeeds in a context of compassion. Most lawbreakers (especially first time offenders) *want* to confess their 'sins,' work through their guilt and experience the healing of forgiveness. Unfortunately, very few are ever given the opportunity to face those whom they've hurt in one way or another and to ask for and receive forgiveness from them.

"The third step should be to give law-breakers an opportunity to make **Restitution** to those whom they have hurt when and where possible. For example, why lock somebody up who has stolen a woman's purse, but who has recognized his or her misdeed, repented of it and is willing to go to work to repay the lady what s/he has deprived her of? I'm convinced that thousands of people, who we now force to sit in degrading prisons, would be grateful for this kind of opportunity and would learn far more from it in terms of building a constructive future than they do by remaining in jail and building up internal resentment and frustration.

"The final step should be to give the law-breaker who has benefitted from the above the kind of supportive 'after-care' that will help him or her to re-enter society as a **Renewed** person. At present, people who've gone to prison carry a stigma with them for the rest of their lives that hampers their future positive development and opportunities. They have difficulty getting jobs, in assuming civic duties, in being accepted as people whose mistakes are behind them. We must do more to prepare ex-convicts to face this challenge creatively and, at the same time, educate the public to stop demanding retribution and start supporting reformation for these people. I'm convinced that if our penal institutions approached their treatment of criminals in this way, there would be fewer of them, the crime rate would once again go down, and the enormous costs of supporting our present penal system would be reduced.

"Thank you once again for this opportunity to address you on this matter."

****

If you were a member of this Rotary Club and heard this speech, what would your reaction be?

The Lifestyle of Jesus

On the night Judas betrayed Jesus, the Gospels record that most of the disciples deserted him and fled out of fear for their own lives. With only two exceptions, they then went into hiding until Jesus appeared to them "behind closed doors" after his resurrection. The two exceptions were Peter and John. Instead of running, they followed the arresting party at a safe distance until they ended up in the courtyard of the High Priest's residence in the middle of the night.

John apparently had some connections to a priestly clan and boldly went in to see what would become of Jesus. (He would later also bravely appear at the foot of Jesus' cross when he was executed). This left a, for once, terrified Peter outside the gate on his own. John sent somebody to let him into the courtyard where he warmed himself beside a fire that the guards had built there.

During the course of his conversation with the guards and servants, he was accused of being one of Jesus' disciples three times - an accusation that, in order to save his own skin, he vehemently denied. Just as Jesus was being led along a balcony that looked down over the courtyard, a rooster crowed. Jesus looked down at Peter and he looked up at him, suddenly remembering that Jesus had predicted that when the crunch came, brave, boisterous Peter would deny him.

Peter, now a man with a broken heart, went back out of the gate sobbing into the night. He had failed his Lord and Master, and now that Lord and Master, as he had predicted a number of times, was being led away to a night of trial and tribulation that would eventually end in an agonizing death.

Three days later, Peter and the other disciples were stunned by several encounters with the risen Christ - one of them involving only Peter and the Lord. What did they say to each other? We don't know, but we can guess. Did Jesus berate Peter for denying him? Not likely. More likely, Peter must have asked for forgiveness for deserting and denying Jesus on that black night - and Jesus must have forgiven him. However, even so, how could Jesus ever again trust Peter to be a loyal disciple, let alone a leader in the church, when he would be subjected to the inevitable pressures that were sure to come?

Some weeks later, Peter, James and John and some of the other disciples had left Jerusalem for the safer territory of Galilee. They'd gone back to their old business of fishing on Lake Galilee. Suddenly, after a stranger on the beach told them where to catch a huge school of fish after they'd caught nothing all night, they knew that it was the Lord. Peter jumped out of the boat and rushed to the beach while the other disciples dragged the great catch of fish to the shore.

After they had eaten breakfast together, Jesus had a little side conversation with the repentant Peter. He made it clear that he was going to give him another chance when he charged him with taking care of his 'sheep.' (See John 21:1-13)

To those who repent of their sins, their mistakes, their failures, their errors, Jesus demonstrates that the God of grace is always the God of the second chance - and the third chance - and the fourth chance. And that is the way he wants his followers to be with others as well - constructive people who look for the good in others, are happy when they find it and sad when they don't. Like Jesus, a constructive person will think first about helping an offender repent and begin anew knowing that compassion will bring about change in another person quicker than condemnation.

On another occasion, the Pharisees brought a woman to Jesus who had been caught committing adultery. They were intent on stoning her to death as the Law of Moses demanded. Trying to trick him, they asked him his opinion. Jesus bent down, wrote some squiggle in the dust, then straightened up and startled them by saying, "Let him who is without sin among you cast the first stone." (John 8:7) The wiser, older men immediately got the point - a constructive person will remember her or his own sins when dealing with the sins of others and be merciful - and walked away chagrined.

It took the younger men a little longer to admit that Jesus had a point, but they too eventually left until all of her accusers were gone. Did this mean that Jesus condoned adultery; that he more or less said, "Well girls will be girls"? Of course not. He told the obviously repentant woman that he did not condemn her, but that neither did he condone what she had done. She should "Go and sin no more." (See John 8:1-11)

When it comes to the question of retribution or reformation, Jesus always came down on the side of reformation, and he expects his followers to do the same. A repentant spirit on the part of an offender is a necessary ingredient to renewal, transformation and restoration, but fellow sinners who are unwilling to give others another chance despite their contrite spirit are judgmental when they should be merciful. To such people, Jesus makes it clear that God will use the same yardstick to judge them as they are using to judge and condemn others. (See Matthew 7:1-5)

Does this mean that there are no consequences to pay for evil, sinful acts? Of course not. No matter how repentant and how forgiven a transgressor is, the damage, heartache, suffering and loss caused by the transgressor, and the resultant penalty, need to be dealt with and made right.

For example, the adulteress that Jesus did not condemn would have been expected to mend her relationship with all who were injured by her sinful action. And even though forgiven and healed, like a physical injury made well, there would still be a scar in her heart. Nevertheless, she would be restored and renewed and could resume a joyful, productive life with a grateful spirit. Constructive people will see this as the ultimate goal in helping others start anew.

Making a Point with Haiku Poetry

Try describing a constructive person by using the Japanese Haiku poetry form. It's simple in structure, but not all that easy to write without considerable thought. It consists of three lines of five, seven and five characters (or syllables) respectively.

Examples

**Constructive People
are always compassionate,
never vindictive.**

**Love is Constructive
is joyful about the good,
Sad about evil.**

Building Up or Tearing Down?

1. Name five actions or attitudes that tend to tear other people down and destroy relationships and explain how they do so.

2. Now name five actions or attitudes that tend to build other people up and strengthen relationships and how they do so.

What Does This Tell You About Yourself?

1. "If I were to rate myself from 1-10 on a continuum between being a constructive person or being a destructive person, I would put my mark at ……………

2. "Some things I sometimes do to tear people down are …….

3. "Some things I sometimes do to build people up are ……...

4. "If I could change one thing about myself, I would ……….

Chapter Twelve

A CURE FOR COWARDICE

> **Read All About It!**
>
> Read how two men had the courage to defy a wicked king in 1 Kings 18:1-40.

"We Need the Courage to be Hot or Cold, to Stand for Something Lest We Fall for Anything."

Here are 20 acts of courage by well-known people. Rank them from 1 - 20, with your first choice being what you consider to be the most courageous act and so on. (Look up the names of people you may be unfamiliar with on the Internet).

1. Moses leading the Israelites out of Egypt.

2. Nelson Mandela leading the fight against apartheid in South Africa.

3. Edmond Hillary making the first climb to the summit of Mt. Everest.

4. Abraham Lincoln signing the Emancipation Proclamation.

5. David fighting against the giant Goliath.

6. Martin Luther King, Jr. leading the non-violent civil rights movement.

7. Florence Chadwick swimming the English Channel both ways.

8. Abraham leaving his home in Haran for a land he had never seen.

9. Charles Lindberg making the first solo flight across the Atlantic Ocean.

10. Jackie Robinson becoming the first African American to play major league baseball.

11. Madam Curie risking death in order to perfect the use of radium.

12. Francis of Assisi turning his back on wealth and ease to live a simple life of obedience, chastity, and poverty.

13. Florence Nightingale serving as the first nurse near a battlefield under horrible conditions in the Civil War.

14. Jesus Christ preaching against the Jewish religious establishment even though he knew it would ultimately mean his certain death.

15. Franklin Roosevelt becoming President of the United States with his legs paralyzed.

16. Paul and Silas singing hymns at midnight after they'd been arrested, beaten, and thrown into prison.

17. Neil Armstrong making humankind's first journey to the moon.

18. Mahatma Gandhi leading the non-violent movement to gain India's independence from the British.

19. Mother Teresa ministering to the poor, sick and dying people of Calcutta.

20. General Dwight Eisenhower making the decision to launch the World War II D Day invasion of Nazi occupied Europe.

Explain why you chose what you did for #1, 2 and 3, and why you chose what you did for #18, 19 and 20.

The Lifestyle of Jesus

One Sabbath day, Jesus met a man who'd been born blind sitting by the side of the road begging. Jesus spit on the ground, made some mud paste, rubbed it on the man's eyes and told him to wash his face in the Pool of Siloam so he would be able to see again. The man believed what Jesus said, went to the pool, washed his face and, for the first time in his life, could see!! His neighbors and the people who had seen him begging before this, asked, "Isn't this the man who used to sit and beg?" Some said, "He is the one," but others said, "No he isn't; he just looks like him." So the man himself said, "I'm the man." "How is it that you can now see?" they asked him. He answered, "The man called Jesus made some mud, rubbed it on my eyes, and told me to go to Siloam and wash my face. So I went, and as soon as I washed, I could see." (See John 9:8-11)

Then they took the man to the Pharisees to have the miracle authenticated. But the Pharisees were very upset that Jesus had cured the man on the Sabbath, since they interpreted any such act as 'work', which was strictly forbidden on the holy day. They again asked the man how he had received his sight. He told them, "He put some mud on my eyes; I washed my face, and now I can see." Some of the Pharisees said, "The man who did this can't be from God, for he doesn't obey the Sabbath law." Others, however, said, "How could a man who's a sinner perform such miracles as these?" And they were divided. So the Pharisees asked the man once more, "You say he cured you of your blindness - well, what do you say about him?" "He's a prophet," the man answered. (See John 9:15-17)

But they weren't willing to believe that he'd been blind and could now see, so they called his parents and asked them, "Is this your son? You say that he was born blind; how is it, then, that he can now see?" His parents were afraid of the Jewish authorities, who had already agreed that anyone who said he believed that Jesus was the Messiah would be expelled from the synagogue. So they answered, "We know that he's our son, and we know that he was born blind, but we don't know how it is that he's now able to see. Neither do we know who cured him. Ask *him*; he's old enough, and he can answer for himself!" (See John 9:19-22)

Now the pressure was really on. They called the man who had been born blind back and said to him, "Promise before God that you will tell the truth! We know that this man who cured you is a sinner." He courageously answered, "I don't know if he's a sinner or not. One thing I *do* know: I was blind, and now I see!" They asked him again about his cure with the obvious intent of getting him to recant what he'd just said. But he bravely threw down the gauntlet: "I've already told you and you wouldn't listen. Why do you want to hear it again? Maybe you, too, would like to be his disciples!" They were enraged and insulted him. "*You* are that fellow's disciple; but *we* are Moses' disciples. We know that God spoke to Moses; as for that fellow, however, we don't even know where he comes from!" (See John 9:24-29)

The man screwed up his courage and answered,

> "What a strange thing that is! You don't know where he comes from, but he cured me of my blindness! We know that God doesn't listen to sinners; he does listen to people who respect him and do what he wants them to do. Since the beginning of the world nobody has ever heard of anyone giving sight to a person born blind. Unless this man came from God, he wouldn't be able to do a thing!" They answered, "You were born and brought up in sin - and you are trying to teach *us*?" (John 9:30-34)

(Their theory was that anything bad that happened to a person must have been caused by his or his parents' sin). And they expelled him from the synagogue. When Jesus heard what had happened, he found the man and asked him if he believed in him. The man said he did and knelt down before Jesus. (See John 9:35-38)

Here was a man who had the courage to do the right thing even though it was a very unpopular thing that would result in dire consequences.

Abraham was one of the great heroes of the Christian faith. Here's what the writer of Hebrews has to say about him.

> "It was faith that made Abraham obey when God called him to go out to a country which God had

promised to give him. He left his own country without knowing where he was going. By faith he lived as a foreigner in the country that God had promised him... It was faith that made Abraham able to become a father, even though he was too old and Sarah herself could not have children. He trusted God to keep his promise. Though Abraham was practically dead, from this one man came as many descendants as there are stars in the sky, as many as the numberless grains of sand on the seashore." (Hebrews 11:8-12)

However, on several occasions, even Abraham didn't have the courage to live by his convictions. One time, when there was a famine in Canaan, he took his family and his whole entourage to Egypt. Instead of relying on God's protection while he was there, he told his wife Sarah (who was very beautiful) to pass herself off as his sister so that the Egyptians wouldn't kill him and steal his possessions in order to get his wife. (This was somewhat of a 'white lie' since she actually was his half-sister). This got him into big trouble when the King of Egypt took a fancy to Sarah and added her to his harem! Had God not intervened, this could have been a disaster for Abraham and Sarah and endangered God's whole plan to raise up a chosen people who would trace their ancestry back to them. (See Genesis 12:12-20)

One would think Abraham would've learned his lesson and would've had more courage to tell the truth the next time this temptation came along. But he didn't! On another occasion, he and Sarah had to temporarily move to Philistia and the same thing happened. He told the same half truth and King Abimelech added Sarah to *his* harem! Only another intervention by God saved the day. (See Genesis 20:1-18)

These incidents in the life of Abraham show that even the strongest Christian can be tempted to be a coward rather than to be courageous. To have courage means to do the right thing when you're tempted to do the wrong thing.

Jesus not only *taught* his followers to be courageous, especially when faced with attacks from evil forces, but *demonstrated* it in a way that no one else has ever done before or since. Paul succinctly sums it up in his letter to the Philippians.

> "He always had the nature of God, but he did not think that by force he should try to remain equal with God. Instead of this, of his own free will he gave up all he had, and took the nature of a servant. He became like a human being and appeared in human likeness. He was humble and walked the path of obedience all the way to death - his death on the cross." (Philippians 2:6-8)

And again in his letter to the Romans.

> "For when we were still helpless, Christ died for the wicked at the time that God chose. It's a difficult thing for someone to die for a righteous person. It may even be that someone might dare to die for a good person. But God has shown us how much he loves us - it was while we were still sinners that Christ died for us! By his blood we are now put right with God; how much more, then, will we be saved by him from God's anger! We were God's enemies, but he made us his friends through the death of his Son." (Romans 5:6-10)

The tremendous struggle that Jesus, the Son of *God*, went through in order to courageously offer his life as a sacrifice for the sins of the world can be seen in his last few hours as a free man before his arrest in the Garden of Gethsemane.

"Grief and anguish came over him. He went off from his disciples about the distance of a stone's throw, threw himself face downward on the ground and prayed. 'My Father, if it's possible, take this cup of suffering from me! Yet not what I want, but what you want'....In great anguish he prayed a second time even more fervently; his sweat was like drops of blood falling to the ground. When he returned to his disciples, he said to them, 'The sorrow in my heart is so great that it almost crushes me. Stay here and keep watch with me.' Once more Jesus went away and prayed, 'My Father, if this cup of suffering cannot be taken away unless I drink it, your will be done.'" (Matthew 26:36-43. See also Luke 21:39-46)

This is the kind of courage that Jesus calls his followers to have in our times of trial - the courage to say or do the right thing no matter what it costs. Courageous people are prudent in that they don't take unnecessary risks or do what's foolish, but when the chips are down, they stand by their convictions and are willing to take a risk for the right. They unselfishly face, rather than try to escape from, difficult circumstances and consequences.

How do we 'screw up' such courage?

- ❖ By keeping, as much as is possible, out of situations where we know we'll be tempted to be cowards. Some people just ask for trouble when, as the old saying goes, "Fools rush in where angels fear to tread."

- ❖ By taking the time and energy necessary to firmly find and confirm what we believe and why we believe it. The reason why too many Christians too often lose their courage and cave in to the lifestyles and ideas of the culture around them, for example, is because when it comes to a familiarity with the Scriptures and with the foundational doctrines of their faith, they're almost illiterate. They haven't invested in what it takes to "fight on for the faith which once and for all God has given to his people." (Jude 3)

- ❖ By caring more about what's right than about what other people think. No matter what our age, peer pressure is one of the most powerful incentives to be cowardly rather than courageous. The Chinese people have a proverb to describe spineless people who are always swayed by what others think. They're like the big half of a watermelon when it's sliced in two. They always go with the bigger half. They're the kind of people that always look around the room to see who has put their hand up before daring to raise their own.

- ❖ By thinking about the consequences of cowardice for ourselves and for others. If *we* don't speak up for the right, who then will? If *we* don't act, who then will? Edmund Burke once said, "The only thing necessary for the triumph of evil is for good men (and women) to do nothing."

Here are a few other statements that people have made about courage.

- ❖ "We can't discover new oceans unless we have the courage to lose sight of the shore."

- ❖ "Behold the turtle that makes progress only when he sticks his neck out."

- ❖ "A ship in the harbor is safe, but that's not what ships are built for."

❖ "We need serenity to accept what can't be changed, courage to change what should be changed and wisdom to distinguish the one from the other."

Peter, Paul and Gerry

Here's the dialogue from six more amusing conversations between Peter, Paul and Gerry. Carefully read through each one and identify the point that it's making.

1. Peter and Gerry are on the baseball field. Peter has been elected manager of the team but says to Gerry, "I can't go out there and manage today, Gerry. I'm no good as a manager. I'm scared to death." Gerry retorts, "*Scared?* Why, you dope!" She launches into a lecture. "You *wanted* to be the manager and now you're going to *be* the Manager!" She gives him a kick in the rear and shouts, "*Now you get out there and manage the team!!*"

   Peter arrives at the mound where the pitcher and the catcher are anxiously waiting, and the catcher says, "Hi, Pete! Where've you been? We've been waitin' for you." Gerry joins the powwow with a bat in her hand and a frown on her face, and Peter says, "Well, at first I thought I probably wouldn't be able to make it, but I finally decided to come out here under the influence of influence."

2. Peter stands on a tree stump with a large parachute spread out on the ground behind him and tied to his back. He's looking scared out of his wits. Gerry stands behind him and thinks to herself, "Just what I thought. He's getting cold feet." She then calls out to Peter, "All you have to do is jump off that stump and float gently to the ground." With a

great shout of "**HEAVE HO!**" she pushes him off the stump. He falls flat on his face with a WUMP! and lays there mumbling into his hat. Gerry walks away saying, "I think I'd better go home and watch some television."

3. Paul is frantically pulling his scarf out of a trash bin hollering, ***GIVE ME BACK THAT SCARF!!*** He turns and says to Gerry, "Nobody's gonna cure me of *anything*! Who are *you* to tell me what to do!? Who is *Grandpa* to tell me what to do!?" He continues, "When *Dad* tells me it's time to stop dragging this scarf around and sucking on my thumb, then I'll do it, but it's nobody else's business. ***Do you understand!?***" Peter, who is standing there, shouts "**Hoorah!**" Gerry tells him to "Shut up!" Paul walks away hugging his scarf and saying to it, "Are you okay ol' buddy?"

4. Paul is sitting in a big lounge chair in the living room looking worried. He says to Peter, "Gerry volunteered me to sing 'Santa Claus Is Comin' to Town' at the Sunday School Christmas program." He gets up and with a terrified look on his face says, "I can't sing in front of a crowd! I'm a *terrible* singer! I've *never* been able to sing!" Peter, trying to console him, says, "Don't worry about it. Psalm 98 says, 'Make a joyful noise unto the Lord.'" Paul shouts, ***"THIS IS THE SUNDAY SCHOOL!!"***

5. Peter and Paul are walking along talking. Paul says, "I don't like to deal with problems head on." He continues, "I think the easiest way to solve problems is to avoid them." They stop, and Paul goes on, "This is my personal philosophy." He concludes, "No problem is so huge or so difficult that it can't be run away from!" Peter has a "You've got to be kidding!" look on his face.

6. Peter and Paul are having another of their philosophical talks while they're walking along. Paul says, "Your trouble,

Pete, is that you live by famous quotes and popular sayings." He continues, "You really thought that if you clenched your teeth, it would help you to become a big shot. Well, there's more to it than just clenching your teeth." They stop, and Paul asks, "Pete, do you understand what I'm sayin'?" Peter replies, "Maybe I didn't clench them hard enough…Maybe if I……" Paul looks exasperated and gives a big sigh.

What Does This Tell You about Yourself?

1. Which conversation do you think most expresses your idea of what having courage is all about and why?

2. Which conversation can you most easily imagine yourself being in and why?

3. True or false? "I'm usually a very courageous person." Explain.

4. "Thinking about being a courageous person makes me want to ……………….."

Chapter Thirteen

HONESTY IS THE BEST POLICY

> **Read All About It!**
>
> Read how two people who weren't HONEST paid the consequences in Acts 5:1-11.

A Walk in the Woods: A Parable

Sam was tired. He'd been walking a long way. He stood at a fork in the road. He could see that if he went left, although the path was straight, it would be narrow, rocky and uphill most of the way.

The road to the right was quite different. It was smooth, broad and mostly on the level. It was true that he couldn't see around the first bend, but what did that matter? It had a sign with the same destination on it that the sign on the path did. Both would end up at the same place. Besides, the sign also said 'Short cut.'

Sam had been warned about this 'short cut' road before he'd set out on his hike. He'd heard that it was slippery in some spots and tricky in others, but that didn't bother him. He was sure he could work around that kind of thing, and besides, he was tired and in a hurry to get to where he was going.

He started off on the road to the right, hardly noticing some small additional lettering on the sign which said: "You have just entered Composition Copying Country." Rounding the first bend, he came across a dip in the road filled with a large puddle of rain water. He hesitated, but then took off his shoes, rolled up his pants and waded through. The road was slimy under the water and he almost slipped and fell, but he caught himself and made it to the other side. He didn't notice that someone had traced "The first time is always the hardest" in the mud at the edge of the road.

There were more dips and more puddles as he went along, but Sam didn't slip once as he waded through them. He was getting used to it. He didn't particularly like them, but, he thought, he was, after all, making much faster progress in reaching his destination than if he'd taken the path.

Clouds had been gathering overhead for some time. Sam wasn't too happy about that since he had hoped to finish his hike before it rained and produced even more puddles. However, a slow drizzle now began to fall which shortly developed into a steady rain. Sam got wetter and wetter and more and more uncomfortable as he sloshed along. For a moment it seemed to him as though the raindrops were drumming out a pattern as they hit the pavement - "The Prof suspects you....The Prof suspects you." Sam quickened his pace, his heart beating a bit faster.

Sam was greatly relieved when the rain finally stopped and the sun came out again. His clothes dried out as he walked along and his heart became lighter. But it was now getting later in the after-noon and he began to worry about reaching his destination before dark. "I've been walking quite a long time," he said to himself. "Maybe this road isn't such a great short-cut after all."

He came to a path on the left that wound steeply up a hillside. A small sign read, "Way Back to Honesty Lane." He looked down the main road winding through 'Examination Forest' and thought he could see the tips of the towers of a town in the distance. He'd heard about this dreaded forest. He'd also heard that you could make it to the town very quickly on this road if you dared to cross a narrow suspension bridge over 'Cheating Chasm.' He stood undecided. Should he waste time and go the more difficult way on the path, or should he take his chances on the footbridge?

With a shrug of his shoulders, Sam kept going down the road. He'd made it down this road so far without too much trouble, and he was very tired by now and in a hurry to get to the town. He walked on until he was deep into the forbidding and gloomy forest. The further he went the quicker he walked.

He finally came to the bridge, and it was as scary as he'd been told. With his heart in his mouth he edged out onto it clinging tightly to the guide ropes on either side. He was soon half-way across. His heart was beating wildly! He dared not look down into the yawning chasm below. He shut his eyes tightly and groped his way towards the opposite bank. He didn't notice the missing boards until he was almost to the other side.

With a desperate scream he fell through the hole in the deck of the bridge! He bounced off a rock, rolled down a slope and was stopped by a clump of trees hanging out over the edge of the canyon. He was hurt and frightened and screamed for help. Then he fainted.

He woke up and found himself in bed in a warm cottage. A kindly man was bending over him just finishing putting a splint on his broken arm. "You'll be all right," he said. "You've had a nasty fall. Didn't anyone warn you about that bridge?"

They had a long talk. He told Sam about other people who had made the same mistake. He also told him that the path he'd first come across wasn't nearly as difficult as it looked at first. "Besides," he said. "You feel great after a good climb up that path." Sam sheepishly nodded his head and felt ashamed that he'd settled for what seemed like the easy way.

After a few days of rest, Sam was ready to resume his walk. "I've learned now that short-cuts aren't always the best cuts," he told his new found friend. He headed straight to another little path winding steeply up the hillside that the man had told him about with a sign reading "Way back to Honesty Lane." "Honesty really *is* the best policy," he thought to himself.

****

Think about a time when *you* were tempted to be dishonest. What kind of an ending did that story have?

The Lifestyle of Jesus

Dishonesty comes in many colors. Some people are dishonest by telling lies or half truths to deceive others, often with disastrous consequences. For example, during the early days of the Christian church as described in the book of Acts, wealthy people were helping the poor in their group by selling some of their property and contributing at least some of the proceeds to the church. A man named Ananias and his wife Sapphira sold some property that belonged to them. They agreed to keep part of the money for themselves and turn the rest over to the apostles. This would have been perfectly fine *except* that when Ananias brought the funds to Peter, he lied and told him that he was contributing the whole amount of the sale.

Peter said to him, "Ananias, why did you let Satan take control of you and make you lie to the Holy Spirit by keeping part of the money you received for the property? Before you sold the property, it belonged to you; and after you sold it, the money was yours. Why, then, did you decide to do such a thing? You have not lied to people - you have lied to God!" (Acts 5:3-4)

As soon as Ananias heard this, the shock of being exposed as a fraud in front of the whole community apparently caused him to suffer a stroke or a heart attack, and he fell down dead. When his wife arrived three hours later, not knowing what had happened, she too lied when asked about the contribution they had made. Upon learning that her husband had been exposed and had died as a result, she too dropped dead. (See Acts 5:7-10)

The same thing happens today as well. Especially since the advent of the Internet, it sometimes seems as though, half the world is out to steal from or scam the other half. However, as the old saying goes, "The truth will always out." In other words, sooner or later the perpetrator of a Ponzi scheme or some other scheme will be exposed and will have to face the consequences.

Lying doesn't only have to do with attempting to directly steal things but, like Ananias and Sapphira, also with giving a false impression. We can all remember times when as a child we were tempted to lie or tell a half truth when our parents or our teacher asked "Who did this?" Or when our friends picked on some kid on the playground and we said nothing when we should have stood up for him or her - giving the false impression that we agreed with what they were doing.

Dishonest people aren't only those who attempt to trick others out of their savings or their goods, but also those who steal other people's ideas, writings or compositions. We call it cheating and plagiarism. Others cheat people out of their time by causing them to waste it.

Still others steal other people's reputation when they spread false gossip about them, or falsely malign their character, or lie about them in court. Then there are those who steal people's clean air, clear water, good soil and beautiful scenery by polluting, strip mining, spilling oil and chemicals, selling insecticides that kill bees and birds and the like.

Why are people dishonest?

1. Some are too lazy to do their own work.
2. Others are afraid of the consequences of telling the truth.
3. Some don't value their own feelings or opinions very highly.
4. Others are jealous, greedy, vindictive, or selfish.

Followers of Jesus can make progress in overcoming dishonesty in all its forms since he calls and enables them to work at eliminating the basic causes of dishonesty in their lives.

Take the case of Zacchaeus, for example. Tax collectors in Judea in Jesus' day were despised by the Jewish population. As in every day, nobody liked to pay money to the government, especially when that government was an oppressive regime like the Roman Empire of the 1st century. Also, the tax collectors at that time were *Jews* who were working for the hated Romans. These individuals were viewed as traitors to their own people. People felt that rather than fighting the Roman oppressors, these turncoats were *helping* them - and enriching themselves at the expense of their fellow Jews.

Further, it was common knowledge that these tax collectors cheated the people they collected from. They were rip off artists who by hook or by crook would collect more than required and keep the extra for themselves. And because of their skimming off the top, they were well-to-do which especially rubbed the lower classes the wrong way. They highly resented the injustice of their having to support the tax collectors' lavish lifestyle out of their meager resources.

One day, one of these tax collectors, named Zacchaeus, heard that Jesus was coming to town. Since he was short and couldn't see over the heads of the crowd, he climbed up in a sycamore tree to get a better view. He practically fell out of the tree when Jesus stopped, looked up and commanded him to come down. And he, and the crowd of Jews surrounding them, almost fainted when Jesus said he was going to stay at his house that night! Good people like Jesus weren't supposed to even *talk* to these scum bags, let alone defile themselves by going to their homes and *eating* with them!

Zacchaeus was so moved by this gesture that when Jesus arrived at his home, he welcomed him with great joy. During the meal, Zacchaeus stood up and said to Jesus, "Listen, sir! I will give half my belongings to the poor, and if I have cheated anyone, I will pay back four times as much." Jesus replied, "Salvation has come to this house today, for this man, also, is a descendant of Abraham. The Son of Man came to seek and to save the lost." (See Luke 19:1-10)

What a transformation! Every dishonest person in Judea, and especially every tax collector, who heard about this knew that there was hope for them. They too could become followers of Jesus and give up their old dishonest ways of doing things. In fact, another tax collector named Matthew actually did become one of Jesus' twelve closest disciples! (See Matthew 9:9-10)

Pick a Proverb

Here are twenty sayings out of the book of Proverbs. Read each one and explain the point it is making by re-phrasing the proverb in your own words.

1. Wealth you get by dishonesty will do you no good, but **honest**y can save your life   (Proverbs 10:2)

2. **Honest** people are safe and secure, but the dishonest will be caught. (Proverbs 10:9)

3. The Lord protects **honest** people, but destroys those who do wrong. (Proverbs 10:29)

4. If you are good, you are guided by **honest**y. People who can't be trusted are destroyed by their own dishonesty. (Proverbs 11:3)

5. Riches will do you no good on the day you face death, but **honest**y can save your life. (Proverbs 11:4)

6. **Honest**y makes a good person's life easier, but the wicked will cause their own downfall. (Proverbs 11:5)

7. Righteousness rescues those who are **honest**, but those who can't be trusted are trapped by their own greed. (Proverbs 11:6)

8. **Honest** people will treat you fairly; the wicked only want to deceive you. (Proverbs 12:5)

9. The wicked are trapped by their own words, but **honest** people get themselves out of trouble. (Proverbs 12:13)

10. **Honest** people hate lies, but the words of wicked people are shameful and disgraceful. (Proverbs 13:5)

11. If you are lazy, you will meet difficulty everywhere, but if you are **honest**, you will have no trouble. (Proverbs 15:9)

12. It is better to have a little, **honest**ly earned, than to have a large income, dishonestly gained. (Proverbs 16:8)

13. The Lord wants weights and measures to be **honest** and every sale to be fair. (Proverbs 16:11)

14. It is better to be poor but **honest** than to be a lying fool. (Proverbs 19:1)

15. Be kind and **honest** and you will live a long life; others will respect you and treat you fairly. (Proverbs 21:21)

16. No matter how often **honest** people fall, they always get up again; but disaster destroys the wicked. (Proverbs 24:16)

17. Better to be poor and **honest** than rich and dishonest. (Proverbs 28:6)

18. Be **honest** and you will be safe. If you are dishonest, you will suddenly fall. (Proverbs 28:18)

19. **Honest** people will lead a full, happy life. But if you are in a hurry to get rich, you are going to be punished. (Proverbs 28:18)

20. Evil people are trapped in their own sins, while **honest** people are happy and free. (Proverbs 29:6)

****

Which proverb(s) do you find to be the most challenging for your own life?

Which proverb most appeals to you as a motto for your life?

What Does This Tell You About Yourself?

1. "It's sometimes difficult for me to be honest because……………….

2. "I think an honest person is…………………

3. "The best way to overcome dishonesty is to…………….

4. "I'll try to overcome dishonesty by………………………

Chapter Fourteen

You Forgot to Say "Thank You"

> **Read All About It!**
>
> Read how a man was THANKFUL while sitting in prison in Philippians 4:10-20.

It's All in the Way You Look at It

An eye Doctor once offered two high school kids a pair of 'magic glasses.' One refused and said he didn't like to wear glasses. The other accepted and said she'd try them out and see if they really worked. The following is an account of one day in the lives of these two students.

Doug slowly got out of bed, rubbed his eyes and looked out the window. "Ugh! Rain again!" he thought. "Another depressing day!" He quickly got ready for school, ran downstairs and sat down at the table to eat his breakfast. He looked down at his bowl. "Not Cheerios again!" he muttered. "Can't we ever have something a little different Mom?" he asked a little louder. He hurriedly finished his breakfast and dashed out the door grabbing his book bag on his way out. If he didn't hurry, he'd be late!

He reached the bus stop and waited impatiently in the rain. The buses were as crowded as usual, but he managed to squeeze in just before the door shut on the second one that stopped. "Lousy bus service," he said to himself, "can never get a seat."

Doug arrived at school and hurried to the Assembly Hall. He sighed as the usual announcements were made. "Same old stuff every day," he thought. When the special speaker was introduced, he let his mind wander to other things since he'd long ago decided that most Assembly speakers were hopelessly boring.

He began his classes with the same resigned determination with which he greeted every school day. But his usual routine was interrupted by a rather rude shock in sixth period English. The test paper he received back had a big red 'F' on it! "This teacher really has it in for me!" he seethed. "My paper isn't all that bad. She just nitpicks about everything. Nobody could possibly please her!"

Today was the day for the Stamp Club to meet. Doug sat in the back and listened to the Club Chairman explain the plans the club committee had made for an exhibition. He spoke up. "Why do we have to have another exhibition? It seems like we do the same old thing every year." There was a strained silence as everybody waited for Doug to suggest an alternate plan, but he didn't.

That night, after supper, some T.V. and some studying, Doug lay on his bed thinking over the events of the day. 'I've had better days," he mumbled to himself as he drifted off to sleep.

****

Courtney slowly got out of bed, rubbed her eyes and groped for the new pair of 'magic glasses' that Dr. Wilson had given her the day before. She looked out the window, "It's still raining," she thought. "The garden will love that." She quickly got ready for school and sat down at the breakfast table. She looked down at her bowl and started to say, "Not Cheerios again Mom!" but then caught herself and closed her mouth as she remembered the little migrant kids with empty bowls lining up for UN handouts she'd seen on the news the night before. She hurriedly finished her breakfast and dashed out the door, grabbing her book bag on the way out.

She reached the bus stop and waited under her umbrella. The buses were as crowded as usual, but she managed to squeeze in just before the door shut on the second one that stopped. "Well, at least I got in," she said to herself. "It's better than walking."

She arrived at school and hurried to the Assembly Hall. She listened closely to the announcements and was reminded of something she'd forgotten about. "It's a good thing they repeated that," she thought, "or I might have forgotten all about it." When the special speaker was introduced, she paid close attention to what she said. Some speakers were pretty boring, but some were very interesting. And even with the boring ones, she'd decided long ago that if you tried hard enough, you could at least get something worthwhile out of what they said.

She began her classes thinking how lucky she was to be in school when so many other kids in the world were languishing in refugee camps. When she arrived at her sixth period English Class, she received a rather rude shock. The test paper she received back had a big red 'F' on it! "Well, I've been caught napping," she thought. "I tried to take a shortcut in my preparation, and it backfired. I guess I've learned my lesson. Better now than on the final exam!"

Today was the day for the Stamp Club to meet. Courtney sat in the front row and listened to the Chairperson explain the plans the committee had made for an exhibition. She spoke up. "I'm sure we're all grateful for all the work the committee has done. The plan sounds fine, but perhaps we could add a few new angles so that it would be even better than those in the past." Everybody nodded their heads and a general discussion followed that led to some exciting ideas.

That night, after supper, some studying and some T.V., Courtney took off her glasses and lay on her bed thinking over the events of the day. "This has been a good day," she said to herself, "lots to be grateful for. I think I'll wear these glasses again tomorrow!"

****

Explain what 'magic' these glasses had. What do people mean when they say that people go through life looking at the same glass, but some see it as being half empty, while others see it as being half full?

The Lifestyle of Jesus

Every child grows up with "You forgot to say thank you" ringing in his or her ears. It seems that even after we've grown up, gratitude for some act of kindness, some generous gift, some neat compliment, some kind of blessing doesn't come automatically.

Even though he had to contend with a lot of difficulties, Jesus modeled a life of on-going gratitude. He always gave thanks for his meals and never took them for granted. For example, before he fed the multitudes, he looked up to heaven and gave thanks to God. (See Matthew 14:19; 15:32-38)

Even at the Last Supper, when he was facing imminent betrayal and crucifixion, he didn't forget to thank his Father in Heaven for the food they were about to eat. (See Luke 22:19) And then after his resurrection, we find him with two of his followers at their home in Emmaus where, Luke says, "He sat down to eat with them, took the bread, and said the blessing; then he broke the bread and gave it to them." (Luke 24:30)

Jesus also expressed his thanks to his Father in Heaven for listening to his prayers and answering them. Before he raised his friend Lazarus from the dead, "Jesus looked up and said, 'I thank you Father that you listen to me. I know that you always listen to me, but I say this for the sake of the people here, so that they will believe that you sent me.'" (John 11:41)

Because of Jesus' example, gratitude became a major theme for his followers. For example, the Apostle Paul, in his great tome to the Romans where he spells out the basic foundations of the Christian life, divides it into three sections - Sin, Salvation and Service or Guilt, Grace and Gratitude. After describing how the human race has failed to live up to what God expects of us and going on to explain how God came in Jesus to once again put us right with himself, he then spends the last part of the letter calling on us to live a life of gratitude to God for all he has done for us. He begins this section by saying,

> "So then, my friends, because of God's great mercy to us I appeal to you: Offer yourselves as a living sacrifice to God, dedicated to his service and pleasing to him. This is the true worship that you should offer. Do not conform yourselves to the standards of this world, but let God transform you inwardly by a complete change of your mind. Then you will be able to know the will of God - what is good and is pleasing to him and is perfect." (Romans 12:1-2)

The rest of the letter spells out in practical detail what this life of gratitude should look like. (See in particular the rest of chapter 12).

Thankfulness is a way of acknowledging an act of loving concern on our behalf, especially when we don't really deserve or haven't earned that concern. We move into a new neighborhood and are welcomed by a neighbor we've never met ringing our doorbell and giving us a freshly baked pie. We're on the side of the road jacking up a flat tire when a stranger stops and offers to help. We walk into a church where we've never been before and somebody asks us over for dinner. We're about ready to leave the office and everybody jumps out and yells "Surprise! Happy Birthday! Come and have some cake and ice cream." How could we not thank people when we're in these or similar situations?

A truly thankful person is grateful for the small and common as well as for the big and extraordinary. After all, when Jesus fed the multitudes, on one occasion he only had five loaves and two fish, but he gave thanks for them - and then look what happened! (See Luke 9:16) The 'little' things in life are often taken for granted, but a thankful follower of Jesus will be grateful for the smallest flower that blooms, for every bird that sings, for the tiniest seed that's planted, for the little cut that heals - for the mundane as well as the magnificent. A thankful person will see every day of life, health, work and play, every friend, every pleasure however small, as a gift from God that should elicit a prayer of thanksgiving.

Gratitude also shows that I recognize the need for others and that I care about others. Once, Jesus healed ten lepers and sent them off to the Temple to show themselves to the priest, be officially declared clean and be welcomed back into the community. All ten were overjoyed to be healed, but only *one*, and a foreigner at that, came back to thank Jesus. (See Luke

17:11-19) By so doing, he acknowledged that it took more than his own bootstraps to pull himself out of a bad situation. And by so doing, he also acknowledged that he now, as a sign of his gratitude, had an obligation to help others to have the same experience.

John Done wrote a famous poem expressing the truth that we all need each other and need to be grateful for each other:

> "No man is an island,
> Entire of itself,
> Every man is a piece of the continent,
> A part of the main.
> If a clod be washed away by the sea,
> Europe is the less.
> As well as if a promontory were.
> As well as if a manor of thy friend's
> Or of thine own were:
> Any man's death diminishes me,
> Because I am involved in mankind,
> And therefore never send to know for whom the bell tolls;
> It tolls for thee."

A truly thankful person will be grateful both in times of adversity and in times of prosperity. Paul sat in a Roman dungeon and yet could write to the Christians at Philippi:

> "Rejoice in the Lord always. I will say it again: Rejoice!....Do not be anxious about anything, but in every situation, by prayer and petition, with thanksgiving, present your requests to God. And the peace of God, which transcends all understanding, will guard your hearts and your minds in Christ Jesus...I have learned to be content whatever the circumstances. I know what it is to be in need, and I know what it is to have plenty. I have learned the secret of being content

in any and every situation, whether well fed or hungry, whether living in plenty or in want. I can do all this through him who gives me strength." (Philippians 4:6-7, 11-13)

American Thanksgiving comes but once a year, and even then it has now become overshadowed by 'Black Friday' which is creeping into 'Black Thursday.' For the followers of Jesus, Thanksgiving is celebrated 365 days of the year. However, it's only truly expressed through what we might call 'thanksliving.' In the Old Testament we read, "O give thanks to the LORD, for he is good; for his lovingkindness is everlasting." (1 Chronicles 16:34) And again, "Enter his gates with thanksgiving, and his courts with praise. Give thanks to him; bless his name." (Psalm 100:4)

In the New Testament, Paul sums it all up in one sentence: "In everything give thanks; for this is God's will for you in Christ Jesus." (1 Thessalonians 5:18)

Thanksgiving Day

Suppose this was Thanksgiving Day. Can you think of ten things you have or that others have done for you that you can be thankful for?

- ❖ Which two items are the most important ones in your list?

- ❖ Do you recall thanking somebody for each of the ten things you thought of?

- ❖ How have you shown your gratitude by what you've done or in the way you've lived?

What Does This Tell You About Yourself?

1. "I wonder why I'm ....

2. "I wonder if I could ....

3. "I wonder how I would feel if I were to ....

4. "I think I'll try to ....

Chapter Fifteen

How Is 'Freedom' Spelled?

> **Read All About It!**
>
> Read how you can be set FREE from what weighs people down in Romans 16:17-23.

A Day in the Life of a Bird

I woke up at the crack of dawn. The first faint rays of the sun were creeping across the horizon and turning the sky into a picture postcard. I ruffled my feathers, hopped up on the edge of the nest and peered out at the lake and woods far below wrapped in the mystery of the morning mist. I breathed in deeply, glad to be alive and able to fly!

"Flying was really my thing. Never a day went by that I didn't soar out into the wide open expanses of the limitless sky and fly and soar and dive and climb to my heart's content. Even the rain didn't dampen my enthusiasm unless, of course, it materialized into a howling storm that forced me to hunker down in my nest near the top of the cliff and ride it out.

"Looking around in all directions to make sure there was no hawk circling far above waiting to pounce on me, or no animal below stealthily slithering up the rocks to snatch the newborns out of my nest, I shoved off and went into a steep dive. I always liked to see how close I could come to the tree tops before pulling up and flashing by some startled squirrel at what must have seemed to him like the speed of light. I pulled up sharply and climbed as fast as my wings would carry me until it seemed as though I would rocket all the way to the sun. I eased over and banked into an ever widening series of circles, letting the wind carry me along like a feather. I exalted in my freedom and in the beauty of the unfolding day.

"Looking down, I spotted a man and his dog walking along the shore looking for a place to fish. How sad, I thought, that other creatures were so tied to the earth. They were like prisoners destined never to know the exhilarating feeling of soaring wherever they wished.

"With a start, I realized that I hadn't checked the nest for awhile. I flew over to it and was relieved to see six little heads poking up screaming for their breakfast. I flew down to the trees and began collecting bugs and insects and other edibles and flew them up to the nest, making trip after trip until their stomachs were full and they were settled down again satisfied and secure.

"'It won't be long till flying lessons begin,' I thought as I watched them perched on the edge of the nest. And then there would be the survival lessons as they learned how to detect and avoid all who would be scheming to bring a swift end to their fragile lives. And finally the long winter migration journey would begin.

"I noticed that part of the nest had become weakened during the gale of the night before. I flew down to the ground and began collecting bits of grass and twigs to repair the damage. Trip after trip finally brought enough material up to finish the job.

"Then it was time to hunt for my own breakfast. I skimmed along the surface of the lake looking for minnows in the shallow water. You had to be fast as lightning to catch those little devils, and it was more work than fun. Then off for some more 'free fly' - dashing and darting, zooming and coasting. Then back to the nest. Feeding time again!

"And so it went throughout the day until I once again stood perched on the edge of the nest taking in the spectacular sky. Only this time the colors were gradually growing dimmer in the distance.

"In the gathering darkness, my mind went back over the events of the day. I thought about the man and his dog, long since gone home, and of my young ones and myself. It was true that I was freer than the man, I thought, but freedom to fly didn't mean freedom to abandon my nest or my young ones.

****

What do you think the bird meant by its last statement?

The Lifestyle of Jesus

Many people think that freedom is doing what they want when, where, how and with whom they want to. Freedom is to be free of all limitations. However, it doesn't take reading a whole lot of history to discover that this is a mirage that leads to social anarchy and personal disaster. *Everybody* must learn to live within limits.

For example, everybody knows that you have to stop for a red light or sooner or later there will be a destructive crash, and even if there isn't, some police officer will be glad to write such a person a ticket with a big fine. And should this be repeated, some judge will also be obliged to suspend such a person's driving license. Everybody also knows that death and taxes are unavoidable. We are all mortal and we all must do our share to finance all the institutions, programs and services that benefit the whole of our society. And *everybody's* time here on earth is limited. All people also have natural, social and legal limitations that curtail their absolute freedom.

If freedom doesn't mean that we can live without restraints then what does it mean?

1. First, like the bird in our story, it means the power to choose to live responsibly. It's not "my way or the highway" as Frank Sinatra once suggested, or "doing my own thing," as so many now say, but the power to voluntarily accept necessary personal restrictions that bring order, joy and meaning to life with others.

2. Second, it means the power to be free from all that subtracts from living meaningfully as a person and living harmoniously in society. For example, a person is free to smoke, do drugs, or drink too much alcohol, but doing so is ruinous to a person's health and well being and the well being of others.

    Or, a person is free to accumulate all the wealth, and the lifestyle that goes with it, that s/he can and ignore the needs of others around him or her, but in the end, such selfishness will warp a person's life and deny others who've not had the same opportunities the basic means to live a productive life. Mahatma Gandhi once said, "The earth has enough resources to satisfy everyone's need, but not enough to satisfy everyone's greed."

3. Third, it means to live within the boundaries that God set for humans in the beginning for productive, fulfilled and meaningful lives. Paradoxically, Old Testament

Scriptures like Psalm 119, for example, make clear that the more we live within those boundaries, the freer we are.

- ❖ "Happy are those whose lives are faultless, who live according to the law of the LORD. Happy are those who follow his commands, who obey him with all their heart." (Psalm 119:1-2)

- ❖ "How can young people keep their lives pure? By obeying your commands." (Psalm 119:19)

- ❖ "Keep me obedient to your commandments because in them I find happiness." (Psalm 119:35)

- ❖ "I will live in perfect freedom, because I try to obey your teachings." (Psalm 119:45)

- ❖ "I find my happiness in obeying your commands." (Psalm 119:56)

- ❖ "The law that you gave means more to me than all the money in the world." (Psalm 119:72)

- ❖ "I have learned that everything has limits; but your commandment is perfect." (Psalm 119:96)

- ❖ "Your word is a lamp to guide me and a light for my path." (Psalm 119:105)

- ❖ "The rules that you have given are completely fair and right." (Psalm 139:138)

- ❖ "Those who love your law have perfect security, and there is nothing that can make them fall." (Psalm 119:165)

Like Psalm 119, Jesus taught that freedom is inseparable from responsibility. In other words, the freer we are, the more accountable we are. As we've noted, he once told a story about a rich landowner whose land produced a bumper crop. This created a problem. His barns weren't big enough to store the huge harvest. What could he do? Since he wasn't about to part with even one bushel without making a profit on it, he decided to tear down his barns and build bigger ones where he could store the grain and *all his other goods* (which tells us that he had hoarded way more than he could use).

Well, as we've seen, he did this and congratulated himself as being a very lucky man who now had all the good things he wanted in order to live 'the good life' for many years. "Take life easy, eat, drink, and enjoy yourself!" he said. "But," Jesus said, "God said to him, 'You fool! This very night you will have to give up your life; then who will get all these things you have kept for yourself?'" And, making his point, Jesus concluded by saying, "This is how it is with those who pile up riches for themselves but are not rich in God's sight." (See Luke 12:16-21)

But even more telling than this story are the remarks he made to his disciples immediately following the story, which bear repeating since in our day, one billion of the world's population live on less than $1.00 a day and 2.8 billion live on less than $2.00 a day. "And so I tell you not to worry about the food you need to stay alive or about the clothes you need for your body. Life is much more important than food, and the body much more important than clothes…So don't be all upset, always concerned about what you will eat and drink…Your Father knows that you need these things. Instead, be concerned with his Kingdom, and he will provide you with these things." (Luke 12:22-23, 29-30)

And just *how* will he provide them? The implication is that he will provide them *through* the jobs and the decent wages that the wealthy landowners, like the one he just described (like us?), could give them and pay them instead of, as was mostly the case at that time (and is increasingly the case in our own time), paying them practically starvation wages and hoarding the profits. And rather than gouging the public for as much as could be squeezed out of them, these same landowners (us?) would not hoard grain to raise prices, but would charge a fair rate. Further, they (we?) would not say "bah humbug" concerning the needs of the poor, but have generous hearts and share out of their abundance.

Jesus also taught that whenever we abuse our freedom, we will be judged for it. He told a story about a rich man who dressed in the most expensive clothes and lived in great luxury every day. Friends of a poor man named Lazarus, who was covered with sores, used to bring him to the rich man's door, hoping he could eat the bits of food that fell from the rich man's table. Even the dogs would come and lick his sores.

The poor man died and went to heaven where he sat down to a great feast next to Abraham. The rich man also died and went to Hades where he was in great pain. He looked up and saw Abraham far away with Lazarus at his side. So he called out and had the temerity to say, "Father Abraham! Take pity on me, and send Lazarus to dip his finger in some water and cool off my tongue, because I'm in great pain in this fire!" But Abraham said, "Remember, my son, that in your lifetime you were given all the good things, while Lazarus got all the bad things. But now he's enjoying himself here, while you're in pain." (Luke 16:24-25)

The point of the story was, of course, that those who abuse their freedom to use all their time and energy to accumulate what it takes to live 'high on the hog' and who shirk their responsibility for those who are less fortunate, will someday not only lose all they have, but will also lose their freedom too. "The first will be last and the last will be first." (Matthew 20:16)

What's the Point?

Read through each of the following statements and identify the main point of each one in your own words, beginning each point with "Freedom is ...." You can obtain more background information on the context surrounding these statements by looking up the Bible references given and reading the section in which each statement appears.

- ❖ The Psalmist writes, "In my distress I called to the Lord; he answered me and set me free. The Lord is with me, I will not be afraid; what can anyone do to me?" (Psalm 118:5-6)

- ❖ Jesus read from Isaiah, "He has sent me to proclaim liberty to the captives and recovery of sight to the blind, to set free the oppressed...." (Luke 4:18)

- ❖ "Jesus said, 'If you obey my teaching, you are really my disciples; you will know the truth, and the truth will set you free.'" (John 8: 31- 32)

- ❖ "Jesus said, 'I am telling you the truth: everyone who sins is a slave of sin. A slave does not belong to a family permanently, but a son belongs there forever.

- ❖ If the Son sets you free, then you will be really free.'" (John 8:34-36)

- ❖ Paul writes, "But now you have been set free from sin and are the slaves of God. Your gain is a life fully dedicated to him, and the result is eternal life." (Romans 6:22)

- ❖ Paul writes, "Yet there was the hope that creation itself would one day be set free from its slavery to decay and would share the glorious freedom of the children of God." (Romans 8:21)

- ❖ Paul writes, "….and where the Spirit of the Lord is present, there is freedom." (2 Corinthians 3: 17)

- ❖ Paul writes, "In the past you did not know God, and so you were slaves of beings who are not gods …. Now, you are God's children as a result of his promise …. Freedom is what we have - Christ has set us free! Stand, then, as free people, and do not allow yourselves to become slaves again." (Galatians 4: 8, 28; 5: 1)

- ❖ Paul writes, "As for you, my brothers, you were called to be free. But do not let this freedom become an excuse for letting your physical desires control you. Instead, let love make you serve one another." (Galatians 5:13)

- ❖ Peter writes, "Live as free people; do not, however, use your freedom to cover up any evil, but live as God's slaves." 1 Peter 2:16)

What three statements do you find most helpful in determining what 'freedom' means, and why?

What Does This Tell You about Yourself?

1. "I'm surprised that………………………………

2. "I've discovered that ……………………………..

3. "I've learned that ………………………………

4. "I'd like to ……………………………………...

Chapter Sixteen

All the World's a Stage

> **Read All About It!**
>
> Read how people who get their ROLE in life confused will pay the price in James 5:1-6.

It's All in the Way You Look at It

Ask the next ten people you meet today, "Why are you here? What's your purpose in life?" Nine chances out of ten, you'll probably leave them speechless or stammering as they grope for an answer. By the way, how would *you* answer that question? Somebody has said: "If you don't know where you're going, you'll probably end up somewhere else." We know from experience that there's more truth than fiction to that!

Picture a cork bobbing along in a river. It bounces off a rock here, a tree branch there, and gets hung up from time to time in a backwater. From the time it's dropped into the water upstream until it ends up in the ocean or gets hung up for good somewhere, it has no influence over its direction and no clue as to its final destination. It just floats along aimlessly, and usually ends up a piece of useless rubbish when it could have had a useful function as a bottle stopper or a bobber on a fishing line. You often can't tell much difference between floating corks and some people, can you? Somebody else has put it a little differently: "If you aim at nothing, you'll hit the mark every time."

A more positive way of discussing this idea would be: "You have to take life as it happens, but you should try to make it happen the way you want to take it."

Ask little children what they want to be when they grow up and you'll usually get immediate answers. One wants to be a fireman, another a policeman, a third a nurse, a fourth a teacher "like my Mommy," etc. When you ask young people that same question, much of that naive certainty has disappeared. Teenagers face all the ambiguities of adult life and many aren't sure what they want to be or do or why they want to be or do it. Some never get over their indecision and more or less fall into doing what comes along for reasons that are never quite clear to them.

But others take advantage of every opportunity they have to find out more about the possible options that are open to them. They make friends with people like school counselors and other adults who are living meaningful lives and who they respect. Slowly and carefully they develop interim and then long range goals, along with a creative flexibility to adjust those goals to present and future realities, and to the unexpected. Years later, it's not surprising to find most of these people doing something similar to what they had aimed at doing, and knowing why they're doing it.

A related question, of course, is whether people are doing what they're doing strictly for themselves or whether they're carrying out their role for the benefit of others as well.

Shakespeare once wrote: "All the world's a stage, and we are the players." There are two kinds of actors: one who plays her or his part to gain the acclaim of the audience; another who plays her or his part to fulfill the audience's desire to experience art at its best. The former might be applauded and get rich; but the latter will be respected and get satisfaction (and perhaps a good bit of money and applause as well).

As we step out on the stage of life to 'play our part,' an important question stares us in the face: "Is what I'm doing now or what I'll be doing in the future aimed at benefitting only me or others as well?" Or to put it another way, "Will I be doing this for dollars and applause, or because it will enrich the lives of others, including my own?"

****

How would *you* answer that question?

The Lifestyle of Jesus

Jesus made clear time and time again, both by his teaching and by his example, that a person's ultimate goal in life should not be to prosper, to enjoy or to rule - but to serve others. As we've seen, the ultimate 'show and tell' of this precept occurred when Jesus did what, in the absence of a slave, none of his disciples wanted to lower themselves to do - wash their dirty feet. (See John 13:1-17)

His was an on-going life of service to others through his tireless preaching, teaching and healing. And most of those 'others' were at the bottom of the Palestinian social scale - tax collectors, prostitutes, poor peasants, beggars and outcasts. His bottom line for a productive, satisfying, meaningful and joyful life was "not to be served, but to serve," even to the point of sacrificing his life to "redeem many people." (Mark 10:45)

He often made it clear that those who strive to be served, to be first, to be great will never experience anything of permanent value, while those who strive to serve others and are not worried about being first or great will enjoy that which will forever be valuable. He lived out the paradoxical principle that 'the more you give away, the more you have.' "Be concerned above everything else with the Kingdom of God and with what he requires of you and he will provide you with all these other things," he said. (Matthew 6:33).

He spelled out what he meant by this in what are often referred to as 'The Beatitudes' in his famous Sermon On the Mount:

> "Happy are those who know they are spiritually poor;
> the Kingdom of heaven belongs to them!
>
> "Happy are those who mourn;
> God will comfort them!
>
> "Happy are those who are humble;
> they will receive what God has promised!
>
> "Happy are those whose greatest desire is
> to do what God requires;
> God will satisfy them fully!
>
> "Happy are those who are merciful to others;
> God will be merciful to them!
>
> "Happy are the pure in heart;
> they will see God!
>
> "Happy are those who work for peace;
> God will call them his children!

> "Happy are those who are persecuted because
> they do what God requires;
> the Kingdom of heaven belongs to them!
>
> "Happy are you when people insult you and persecute you
> and tell all kinds of evil lies against you
> because you are my followers.
> Be happy and glad,
> for a great reward is kept for you in heaven."
> (Matthew 5:3-12)

From Jesus' perspective, whoever serves 'lives,' while whoever seeks to be served 'dies' (in spirit if not in body).

> "If any of you want to come with me, you must forget yourself, carry your cross, and follow me. For if you want to save your own life, you will lose it; but if you lose your life for my sake, you will find it. Will you gain anything if you win the whole world but lose your life? Of course not! There is nothing you can give to regain your life." (Matthew 16:24-26)

If Jesus, who had every right to be served, chose to serve, then all who want to live his lifestyle, but who have no right to be served, have no option but to serve. And in so doing, they discover the true joy of living.

A POEM WITH A MESSAGE

Here's a poem written by Edwin G. Robinson. Read it through carefully and think about its meaning.

Richard Cory

"Whenever Richard Cory went down town,
We people on the pavement looked at him:
He was a gentleman from sole to crown,
Clean favored, and imperially slim.

"And he was always quietly arrayed,
And he was always human when he talked;
But still he fluttered pulses when he said,
'Good-morning,' and he glittered when he walked.

"And he was rich – yes, richer than a king –
And admirably schooled in every grace:
In fine, we thought that he was everything
To make us wish that we were in his place.

"So on we worked, and waited for the light,
And went without the meat, and cursed the bread;
And Richard Cory, one calm summer night,
Went home and put a bullet through his head."

****

1. What are all the things that Richard Cory had 'going' for him?

2. What do you think Richard Cory thought his purpose in life was?

3. "In fine, we thought that he was everything to make us wish that we were in his place." Why did the "people on the pavement" want to trade places with him?

4. "He surely must be happy with everything he's got." (True or False.? Why?)

5. Why do you suppose Richard Cory committed suicide?

6. When Jesus said, "Will a person gain anything if he wins the whole world but loses his life? Of course not! There is nothing he can give to regain his life," what did he mean by this and how does it relate to Richard Cory?

What Does This Tell You about Yourself?

1. "If I had to choose between being Richard Cory or being one of the "people on the pavement" who "went without meat and cursed the bread," I would choose to be .... because ....

2. "In my opinion, the thing that makes life most meaningful and joyful is ….......................................

3. "There are some ways in which I am like Richard Cory in that ………………............................

4. "In my life, I would like to ……………

Chapter Seventeen

USE WHAT YOU'VE GOT!

> ### Read All About It!
>
> Read about various types of ABILITIES that people can have in Romans 12:6-16.

Pictures at an Exhibition

I entered what seemed like an endless hall. There were paintings, posters and prints hung here and there in crazy psychedelic patterns covering the walls and ceiling. I felt a certain panic, and as I looked around, I began to sweat profusely knowing that before leaving this hall, I was going to make decisions that could not be reversed for the rest of my life.

"A large painting hanging from the ceiling caught my eye. It was a portrait of somebody's mouth - wide open! You could look past the large teeth right down the person's throat and see his tonsils! The mouth was obviously opened wide to enable its owner to sing a very high note. 'Singing,' I thought. 'Is being a good singer really important to me?' I'd never had much interest in joining a choir. I looked at my check list and quickly crossed 'singing' out.

"I had taken one whole minute to make that decision! That meant I only had nine minutes to go through the whole hall and make my final choices! I'd been told that I'd never be allowed back in again, nor could I make any changes once I'd left.

"I hurried on past a huge banner that proclaimed in screaming colors: 'WHATEVER YOUR LOT IN LIFE, BUILD SOMETHING ON IT!'

"The next thing to catch my attention was a tiny framed print hung all by itself in the middle of a large yellow circle. It was a picture of an artist working over a canvas on which he was creating an intricate geometric design. I'd always enjoyed drawing since I was a small kid and would be unhappy if I lost that skill.

I looked at my checklist again realizing that I could choose only five out of the long list of skills and abilities on that sheet. My faced flushed with the pressure of decision. Was drawing really *that* important to me? I decided it was and circled it on the sheet. Only four choices left!

"I walked along looking at various pictures. Some were easy to make a quick decision about. I hurriedly crossed these off. Others took more time. I stopped in front of a huge painting in a massive gold frame showing a surgeon performing a delicate heart transplant. I had always wanted to be a doctor, so I circled the item called 'delicate motor skills.' Three choices left. Time was running out!

"I hurried on past another huge psychedelic poster with the words. 'IF YOU HAVE IT, USE IT!' emblazoned in dazzling colors splashed across a huge canvas.

"I stopped before a photo of a cook preparing a delicious array of Swedish meat balls, fried chicken, mashed potatoes, green beans, coleslaw and cherry pie. My mouth watered, but I thought, 'I can really get along without this skill. My Mother cooks for me now, and some day I hope to marry a woman who'll be as good a cook as she is.'

"I was just crossing out 'cooking skills' on my list when a bell rang and a loud voice announced over the loud speaker that I had one minute left to make my choices and that I would then have to leave the hall! I began to dash madly about the hall from one picture to the next in utter panic. Only one minute left to make three choices that would determine my whole future forever!

The pictures started spinning and turning! Lights began flashing! Bells began ringing! The door at the far end of the hall slowly began to open ……..

"I awoke with a start! My alarm clock was ringing loudly! The sun was streaming in the window on my face. I laughed with relief at my silly dream. I wouldn't have to make life-long decisions in 10 minutes after all!

"Still thinking about my dream as I climbed out of bed, I said to myself half aloud, 'I wonder what I'd have finally chosen if I'd really had to?'

****

If you had been trapped in such a hall, what five abilities would you have chosen to have and why?

The Lifestyle of Jesus

Matthew records a story Jesus once told about a wealthy man who was about to leave home on a trip, so he called in his servants and put them in charge of some of his finances. Since they had worked for him for some time, he had noticed how well each of the servants had performed and what their capabilities were. So when he called them in, he put each one in charge of a part of his resources according to his ability. He gave one servant five thousand gold coins, a second two thousand, and a third one thousand. Then he left on his trip.

The servant who had received five thousand coins went at once and invested the money and earned another five thousand. The servant who had received two thousand coins did the same and earned another two thousand. But the servant who had received one thousand coins went off, dug a hole in the ground, and hid his master's money.

After a long time the master returned, called the servants in and settled accounts with them. The servant who had received five thousand coins came in and handed over the other five thousand. "You gave me five thousand coins, sir," he said, "and I've earned another five thousand by investing what you gave me." His master congratulated him on a job well done and because he had done well in managing what he had been entrusted with, the master put him in charge of larger amounts. The same thing happened with the servant who had been given two thousand coins since he had also doubled the money that had been entrusted to him.

Then the servant who had received one thousand coins came in and said, "Sir, I know you are a hard man; you reap harvests where you did not plant, and you gather crops where you did not scatter seed. I was afraid, so I went off and hid your money in the ground. Look! Here is what belongs to you." The master was furious and called him lazy and useless. He told him that the least he could have done would have been to deposit his money in the bank where it would have earned interest. Then he commanded that the money this servant had been entrusted with be taken away from him and given to the servant who he had put in charge of the ten thousand coins. He then ordered a servant to throw the lazy servant out where he would cry and gnash his teeth.

Towards the end of the story, Jesus makes his point when he says: "To every person who has something, even more will be given, and he will have more than enough; but the person who has nothing, even the little that he has will be taken away from him." Jesus wasn't talking about money of course, he was talking about people's talents or abilities or gifts. In other words, like the first two servants, we're to use our God-given abilities to the max and not neglect them like the last servant did. (See Matthew 25:14-30)

When we look at this story, we learn seven invaluable principles about our abilities.

1. *Every* servant was given *some* responsibility. It's the same with our abilities. Too often we hear people say, "I can't do anything." That's not true, of course. *Every* person has been created by God and has been given *some* abilities, usually more than they realize.

2. At the same time, nobody has been given *all* the gifts or talents that can be given. The three servants in the story were each given some of their master's resources. Nobody got everything. In the same way, despite the impression that some people give, every person has some limitations when it comes to their talents.

3. People who use their abilities develop the abilities they have and discover more. The two servants that went to work wisely investing their master's money ended up doubling their investment. So it is with our abilities. The more we use them, the more abilities we discover we have. For example, once somebody learns how to play

one stringed instrument, they discover that it doesn't take too much more work to learn how to play another one. And they have a head start in doing so because while learning to play their first instrument, they've learned how to read music.

4. Those who use their abilities receive the joy of praise, the satisfaction of a job well done, and the challenge of greater responsibility. The two servants that took the risk of investing their master's funds and doubled his money got instant promotions. They enjoyed their master's praise and were given even greater challenges that enhanced their lives by enabling them to use their gifts to the max. They felt like a runner who perseveres in a race, strains to cross the finish line before the other contestants and has the exhilaration of winning the race.

5. Those that don't use their abilities because they're too lazy or too scared to try to do so end up losing the ones they have. The third servant in the story discovered the truth of the maxim: "Use it or lose it." If a piece of machinery stands idle long enough, it begins to rust and becomes a worthless piece of junk. In the same way, somebody who wants to master the piano, no matter how gifted they are, can't just assimilate this ability. They have to practice and practice and practice. If they don't continue to do so, no matter how good they've become at playing, they will eventually lose their ability to do so. So it is with our talents - use them or lose them.

6. Those that don't use their abilities are held responsible for what they *could* have done. There are consequences for the way we live our lives. If we squander our God-given talents because we're too lazy or too scared to use them, there will be consequences. If a brilliant student, for example, rests on his or her laurels and doesn't bother to study or to do his or her homework, there will

come a day when s/he will suffer grade-wise and will miss out on a good job possibility.

7. It's better to have risked and failed than to have never tried at all. The master's anger wasn't so much kindled because the fearful servant didn't make him any money, but because the servant didn't *try* to make him any money. My guess is that even if the servant had tried to invest the funds, but had lost the money, the master would have been willing to forgive him because he would at least have tried. So it is with us. God knows we aren't perfect. If we try to use our gifts, but for one reason or another fail and acknowledge our failures, he will always forgive us and give us another chance.

The Apostle Paul makes clear that we don't just use our abilities to gain fame, goods, power and pleasure for ourselves, but to benefit others as well. He likens the Christian community to a physical body that has many different parts carrying out many different functions, all of which are necessary for the body to function effectively. As Paul points out to the Christians Rome:

> "For just as each of us has one body with many members, and these members do not all have the same function, so in Christ we, though many, form one body, and each member belongs to all the others. We have different gifts, according to the grace given to each of us. If your gift is prophesying, then prophesy in accordance with your faith; if it is serving, then serve; if it is teaching, then teach; if it is to encourage, then give encouragement; if it is giving, then give generously; if it is to lead, do it diligently; if it is to show mercy, do it cheerfully."
>
> (Romans 12:4-8)

Four principles come to mind when we think in this way.

1. Living a meaningful life together means that we depend on others to use their abilities and they depend upon us to use ours. For example, a basketball team absolutely depends on a very disparate group of five players to function successfully. Guards are generally shorter, but faster. Forwards not quite as fast, but they're taller and can more aggressively defend the basket and score closer in. The center is the tallest and controls the basket on defense and close in shots on offense. Everybody contributes. If a team member thinks s/he is a whiz and can do it all alone, the whole team suffers.

   We've all heard the phrase: "Too many chiefs and too few Indians." All members of a team need to contribute to make plays work. It's the same in life, and especially among the Christian community.

2. We shouldn't wish we had the abilities of others, but develop the abilities we have. Some people compare themselves to very gifted people and think they can't contribute much "compared to her!" Others are jealous when other people succeed in areas where they aren't very gifted. God values all gifts and all of his people equally. He wants us to concentrate on what gifts or abilities we *do* have and see them as important to the well-being of the group.

3. Those who have 'ordinary' abilities are just as needed as those who have 'spectacular' abilities. In 1 Corinthians 12: 22-24, Paul makes the point that the parts of the body that are rather ugly (like the inner

organs, for example) or that are beautiful but covered up, are just as important, and maybe even more so, than the parts that are beautiful and visible. The heart and the brain, for example, aren't much to look at but the body is totally dependent on them. Likewise, a humble 'behind the scenes' person is just as, and sometimes even more important, than an 'up front' person.

4. In that same chapter, Paul goes on to say that when people don't use their abilities, all suffer. When they do, all prosper. (See 1 Corinthians 12:26) As the saying goes, "A chain is only as strong as its weakest link." This is also true of a group of people. If somebody, out of fear or laziness or jealously or selfishness "lets the team down," the whole team suffers. Conversely, whenever people conscientiously do their part for the good of the whole, the whole team prospers and everyone benefits.

A Talent Teaser

There are clues and a crossword puzzle on the next two pages listing people in the Bible who had abilities and used them well. See if you can identify them by reading the clues. (You can check your answers by looking up the Bible references given).

Although only one item is listed per person, it's obvious that many of these people had a number of abilities and that they used them all well.

Crossword Puzzle Clues

Across

1. A Good Cook
    (Luke 10:38-40)
4. An Author
    (1 Peter 5:13)
5. A Zoo Keeper
    (Genesis 7:6-10)
6. A Businesswoman
    (Acts 16:14)
9. A Beauty Queen
    (Esther 2:16-17)
10. A Wise Politician
    (1 Kings 5:29-30)
12. A Herdsman
    (Amos 7:14)
16. A Religious Worker
    (Luke 1:5)
17. Astronomers
    (Matthew 2:1-2)
19. A Judge
    (1 Samuel 7:15-17)
21. Construction Foreman
    (Nehemiah 2:11-18)
22. A Musician
    (1 Samuel 16:18-19)
24. A Carpenter
    (Matt. 13:55; Jn. 1:45)
26. A Farmer
    (Genesis 4:2)
27. A Business Man
    (Job 1:1-3)
28. A Hunter
    (Genesis 25:27)

Down

2. A Field Hand
    (Ruth 2:3)
3. A Model Mother
    (Luke 1:39-40, 51-52)
4. A Governor
    (Matthew 27:2)
6. A Doctor
    (Colossians 4:14)
7. A Female Judge
    (Judges 4:4)
8. A Loyal Friend
    (1 Samuel 20:42)
11. A Tax Collector
    (Luke 19:2)
13. Community Organizer
    (Exodus 3:7-10)
14. An Army Officer
    (Acts 10:1)
15. A Gardener
    (Genesis 2:15)
18. A Preacher
    (1 Kings 18-21)
20. A Treasurer
    (John 13:29)
23. An Espionage Agent
    (Joshua 2:1-6, 15-16)
24. A Teacher
    (Matthew 4:23)
25. A Scholar
    (Acts 26:24-25)

The Abilities Puzzle

What Does This Tell You About Yourself?

1. "If I were to be listed in this crossword puzzle in the future, my clue would read something like this......................

2. "I feel good about the abilities I have because ....

3. "Some of my abilities that I haven't used as much as I could have or should have are ....

4. "In the future, I would like to make better use of my abilities to ....…...

Chapter Eighteen

IS 'REPENTENCE' OUT OF DATE?

> **Read All About It!**
>
> Read how REPENTANCE and rejoicing go together in Luke 15:1-7.

Simple Words That Are Hard to Say

The high school Principal suddenly appeared at the classroom door. The boys made a mad scramble to get back to their seats. A strained silence fell over the room. The principal looked at the board covered with rhymes and sayings, some of them with rather risqué meanings. "Who wrote these on the board?" he asked in stern tones. Nobody moved. There was total quiet. "I asked, who wrote these on the board?" he repeated slowly. Still silence. "All right, everybody put your hands on your desks palms up."

He walked from desk to desk closely examining the hands and clothes of each student. Every student who had the tell-tale evidence of chalk dust on his hands was asked to go to the Principal's office immediately.

The Principal walked into his office and began the interrogation of the unhappy chalk dust group. It didn't take him long to separate those whom he thought were innocent from the guilty. Only the guilty knew that a few of the 'innocents' who were now leaving his office had succeeded in lying their way out of difficulty!

The Principle concentrated on one of the few that remained. "Why did you do such a thing?" he demanded of one student. The student shifted his feet and stammered out a reply. "I wasn't the only one who did it sir."

He tried again with another one, "What do you have to say for yourself?" "I didn't really want to write anything inappropriate sir," he replied, "but the rest of them laughed at me and said that if I wouldn't, I was a chicken."

"And you?" He turned to a third. The third was known as one of the tougher boys of the school. "All right, I admit that I wrote some of them and that they were a little out of place, but that isn't such a crime, is it? I mean, after all, you were a teenager once too sir. You know that guys like to tell a few shady ones now and then, but that doesn't do anybody much harm. Maybe we shouldn't have written them on a classroom board, but I don't think it's such a big deal."

The Principal's face got a little red, but he held himself in tight control. He looked at the group. "Is that what all of you think?" he asked.

A boy who'd been sitting in quiet distress for a long time spoke up. "Sir …. this is very hard for me to say, but I must …. I know that writing dirty rhymes on the board was a wrong thing to do …. I feel badly that I did it …. and I'm sorry …. I know that it's too easy for boys like me to think dirty about sex …., but I promise you that I'll make a real effort to overcome this temptation in the future …. To show that I mean it, I'll carry out whatever penalty you think best."

People's faces reflected their inner thoughts. The Principal looked relieved. The tough kid had a look of "Why did you have to say *that*?" on his face. The other boys looked like they wished they'd had the courage to say what this boy had said, rather than what they had said.

After further talk and appropriate decisions on the Principal's part, the students returned to their classroom.

****

Do you have a difficult time saying these three simple phrases – "I was wrong;" "I'm sorry;" "I'll change"? What did the boys in this incident, except for the last one, do to avoid having to say them?

The Lifestyle of Jesus

Like our high school friends, there are a number of ways too many people try to avoid facing up to the facts when they've been caught doing or saying something wrong.

1. Some try to lie their way out of it. They don't stop to think that every lie told puts a stain on their character and their reputation. They also don't realize that the more one lies, the easier it is to lie the next time. They think they're too clever to get caught, but, as the old saying goes, sooner or later, "The truth will always out."

2. Others try to excuse themselves by saying they did or said what they did because "everybody else does it." They act as though ethics and morality can be decided by a majority vote. They cave in to peer pressure and follow the crowd. They think that if their actions resemble what a lot of other people think or say or do, they won't be held accountable.

3. Still others try to excuse themselves by distorting the facts or discounting what they did or said as not being all that bad. To them, all behavior is relative. Some is really bad and some is really good, but there's a lot in-between that's grey. People who aren't so self-righteous will know that everybody operates in the grey sometime or other, so what's the big deal?

4. Some try to escape the consequences of their wrongdoing and avoid the uncomfortable prospect of making things right. It takes a lot of courage to say, "I did it. I'm sorry. How can I make it right?"

5. Others will try to do it again if they think they might be able to get away with it. Before long, a behavior that began as something unusual becomes a habit. And they never seem to learn that you can't get away with it all the time. Sooner or later, there will come a day of reckoning.

On the other hand, if people truly repent of their wrongdoings, they'll confess what they've done wrong and ask for forgiveness from those they've wronged. They'll be willing to accept the consequences of their wrongdoing and make things right with those they've wronged as far as is possible. They'll change their behavior so they won't repeat the offence and will show by their actions that they've changed.

Of course, saying "sorry" and changing one's life to reflect that "sorry" are two different things. This was the burden of John the Baptist's message. When he launched a great revival in Judea to call people to repentance and to baptize them as an indication that they had been washed clean of their sin, the Pharisees sent some of their party to investigate what was going on. The Pharisees were known for their self-righteous piety. They kept petty religious rules but avoided true love for God and their neighbors.

John railed at them. "You snakes - who told you that you could escape from the punishment God is about to send? *Do those things that will show that you have turned from your sins.*" (Matthew 3:7-8) His message made it clear that the acid proof that one has truly repented is not what one *says*, but what one *does*. The word 'repentance' doesn't merely mean to be sorry for something, but to change one's mind, one's attitude and one's behavior – to go in a new direction.

This was also Jesus' message. As we've seen in his story about the lost sons, the joy of forgiveness can't be realized until the reality of repentance is demonstrated. It must be more than mere words. It must be accompanied by repentant acts.

In that same story, we also learn that it's not possible to truly make things right with others until we've also made things right with God. The son says to his father, "I have sinned against God and against you." (Luke 15:21) The two are interconnected. Only when we face up to our sins before God and ask for his forgiveness can we have his strength to change our course and the courage to make things right with those whom we've offended.

Take Your Pick

Which do you think is the right answer for each of the following statements? Check the Bible passage listed to see if you're right.

1. John the Baptist was mainly concerned that:

   a. People need to feel guilty when they've done wrong,

   b. People need to say they're sorry when they've done wrong,

   c. People need to do something to demonstrate that they're sorry for having done wrong,

   d. None of these.

   (See Matthew 3:7-8)

2. The word 'repentance' means:

   a. To be upset about doing something wrong,

   b. To turn from doing wrong to doing right,

   c. To offer a special gift to God to show sorrow for sin,

   d. All of these.

   (See Ezekiel 18:30-32)

3. Jesus called people to repent and:

   a. Believe the Good News,

   b. Get ready to be punished,

   c. Obtain forgiveness for their sins by doing good deeds,

   d. Promise that they'd be good.

   (See Mark 1: 14-15)

4. In Jesus' story about the two sons, the key words that

teach us a great deal about the meaning of repentance are:

a. He "changed his mind,"

b. He "went,"

c. He "did,"

a. All of these.

(See Matthew 21: 28- 32)

5. One of the main reasons why some people won't repent is because:

a. They think God has judged them unfairly,

b. They don't think what they did is all that bad,

c. They think they can escape the consequences,

d. They're stubborn and don't want to turn away from their sins.

(See Jeremiah 5:3)

6. In his story about the two sons, one of the things that Jesus teaches us about repentance is:

a. That the joy of forgiveness can be realized whether we repent or not,

b. That making things right with people can't be separated from making things right with God,

c. That the younger son needed to repent more than his older brother did,

d. That doing wrong doesn't bring any bad consequences as long as you say "sorry."

(See Luke 15: 8)

7. A truly repentant person is one who is:

    a. Honest,

    b. Saddened

    c. Humbled

    d. All of these.

    (See Psalm 51)

8. A person who truly repents:

    a. Buries his or her guilt until s/he forgets about it,

    b. Feels that s/he will probably make the same mistake again,

    c. Wishes s/he hadn't been caught,

    d. Knows the joy of complete forgiveness.

    (See Luke 15:20)

9. A person who truly repents:

    a. Keeps from making the same mistake again so that s/he can avoid another punishment.

    b. Never says anything to anybody about it because it's too embarrassing.

    c. Is motivated to change his or her ways out of a sense of gratitude for forgiveness.

    d. Keeps berating him or herself about have sinned and made a mistake.

    (See Psalm 32:1-5)

What Does This Tell You About Yourself?

1. "I usually feel guilty about and need to repent of (lots of things, some things, a few things, nothing) in my past.

2. "I find it (easy, difficult, not so difficult) to repent – to turn away from doing wrong.

3. "I've (often, sometimes, seldom, never) confessed my sins to God and asked for his strength to help me not repeat them.

4. "I've (often, sometimes, seldom, never) confessed my sins to people I've wronged and asked for their forgiveness.

5. "I (often, sometimes, seldom, never) have difficulty in accepting the consequences of my wrongdoing and making things right as far as I can.

6. As a result of thinking about myself like this, I need to …….

Chapter Nineteen

A FORMULA FOR JOYFUL LIVING

> **Read All About It!**
>
> Read how JOYFUL people express themselves in Psalm 100.

Joyful Jingles

Here are a number of statements about the human emotion of joy. Think about each one and see if you can express in one sentence what you think each statement is saying.

1. Joy is like a butterfly. The more you chase it, the more it will elude you. But if you turn your attention to other things, it comes and softly sits on your shoulder.

2. Very little is needed to make a joyful life.

3. I saw rain drops on a river, Joy is like the rain, Bit by bit the river grows, 'til all at once it overflows. Joy is like the rain.

4. To be joyful, you must forget yourself.

5. The gospel in one word is joy.

6. Joy is not always measured in smiles.

7. Happiness and joy are not the same. The one depends on what happens to you, and the other on what happens within you.

8. Joy is like a cork on the waves - unsinkable.

9. Joy is like the common cold - it's catchable.

10. Joy and soda have one thing in common - they both bubble over.

11. Joy is like a plant whose leaves may be withered by the sun, but whose roots live on for another day.

12. Joy, like the other fruit on the tree of life, takes time to ripen.

13. Joy comes to those who don't try to buy it.

14. Joyful people are those who aspire to inspire before they expire.

****

1. Which three jingles do you like the best and why?

2. Try writing a jingle of your own about joy.

3. In our world today, 'joy' seems to be becoming an ever rarer commodity. Glance through today's news items on your computer, for example, and see how many times you can find the word 'joy' or its derivative.

4. How would you suggest we could put a little more joy not only into our news items, but also into our lives?

The Lifestyle of Jesus

People feel happy when their circumstances and experiences are pleasant. They enjoy going on a cruise or having a vacation, for example. They feel good when they're prosperous and don't have to worry about bills or debts or running out of money. They're glad when they're fortunate - when, for example, they win a prize or a nomination or get a good deal on a house or a car. They're content when their relationships are going well, when others love and like them and they love and like others.

They're proud when people recognize their abilities and thank them for their contributions. They're glad when the weather is nice and they can go fishing or out on a picnic in a beautiful setting. They feel great when they can enjoy a good meal in a fine restaurant or a yummy ice cream sundae on a hot day. They're grateful when they're in good health and have plenty of get up and go. They're happy when they have a job or a career that they enjoy.

Feeling joyful can include all of this. But what happens when our circumstances change - when our health begins to fail, the weather is lousy, our finances aren't very good, our job becomes a victim of technology, our relationships run into problems, or our prospects for the career we had hoped to have fade? We then wouldn't probably be too happy, but we can still be joyful because joy doesn't depend on our circumstances, but on inner qualities called peace, love, hope and faith. In other words, happiness depends on our external circumstances while joy depends on the internal quality of our lives.

For example, some of the first Christians had to contend with some awful conditions but were nevertheless radiant with joy. Take Paul and his companion Silas for example. When they visited the city of Philippi and shared the Christian message with the people there, some responded by stirring up a mob and hauling them before the local authorities. Their clothes were ripped off, they were flogged and then they were arrested and thrown into prison where they were chained up in a dark dungeon with their feet in stocks!

What would you do under those circumstances? The account in Acts says that as late as midnight, Paul and Silas were praying and *singing hymns*! (See Acts 16:16-34)

Paul travelled all over the Middle East proclaiming the message about Jesus, the risen Christ and the Savior of the world. Almost every place he went, there were those that believed and became Christians, but there were many who did not and who stirred up mobs to attack him, beat him and jail him. He describes what he went through in one of his letters to the Christians in Corinth.

> "I have been in prison....I have been whipped....I have been near death....Five times I was given the thirty-nine lashes by the Jews; three times I was whipped by the Romans; and once I was stoned. I have been in three shipwrecks, and once I spent twenty-four hours in the water. In my many travels I have been in danger from floods and from robbers, in danger from my own people and from Gentiles; there have been dangers in the cities, dangers in the wilds, dangers on the high seas, and dangers

from false friends. There has been work and toil; often I have gone without sleep; I have been hungry and thirsty; I have often been without enough food, shelter, or clothing." (2 Corinthians 11:23-27)

So you would think Paul would have been a pretty depressed guy, right? Not at all. In that same letter to the Corinthians, he writes, "We are often troubled, but not crushed; sometimes in doubt, but never in despair; there are many enemies, but we are never without a friend; and though badly hurt at times, we are not destroyed....We never become discouraged. Even though our physical being is gradually decaying, yet our spiritual being is renewed day after day." (2 Corinthians 4:8-9, 16)

He continues,

"In everything we do we show that we are God's servants by patiently enduring troubles, hardships, and difficulties. We have been beaten, jailed, and mobbed; we have been overworked and have gone without sleep or food....We are honored and disgraced; we are insulted and praised. We are treated as liars, yet we speak the truth; as unknown, yet we are known by all; as though we were dead, but, as you see, we live on. Although punished, we are not killed; although saddened, we are always glad; we seem poor, but we make many people rich; we seem to have nothing, yet we really possess everything."
(2 Corinthians 6:4-5, 8-10)

Even through the worst circumstances one can imagine, he can still write, "Although saddened, we are *always* glad." In other words, he always had a wellspring of joy carrying him through whatever life threw at him.

In his letter to the Christians in Philippi, he writes,

> "May you always be joyful in your union with the Lord. I say it again: rejoice! .... Don't worry about anything, but in all your prayers ask God for what you need, always asking him with a thankful heart. And God's peace, which is far beyond human understanding, will keep your hearts and minds safe in union with Christ Jesus."
>
> (Philippians 4:4, 6-7)

In fact, in this relatively short letter, Paul uses the word 'joy' in one form or another 15 times! Where was he when he wrote this letter? In a Roman prison! How was he able to be such a joyful person even though he went through so many difficulties? Because he believed what Jesus had promised him and continued to be open to God's Spirit to fill him with joy.

And what did Jesus promise him .... and continues to promise us? "These things have I spoken unto you, that my joy might remain in you, and that your joy might be full." (John 15:11)

How can this happen?

1. If we have a personal relationship with him. "Remain united to me, and I will remain united to you. A branch cannot bear fruit by itself; it can do so only if it remains in the vine. In the same way you cannot bear fruit unless you remain in me." (John 15:4-5)

2. If we pay attention to his teaching. "If you remain in me and my words remain in you, then you will ask for anything you wish, and you shall have it." (John 15: 7)

3. If we obey his commandments. "If you obey my commands, you will remain in my love, just as I have obeyed my Father's commands and remain in his love…. My commandment is this: love one another, just as I love you." (John 15:10, 12)

4. If we bear much fruit (in service to others). "I am the vine, and you are the branches. Those who remain in me, and I in them, will bear much fruit; for you can do nothing without me." (John 15: 14-15).

Pick a Face

Study the following ten photos carefully and decide which face in your opinion most reflects the quality of inner joy. Why did you chose it?

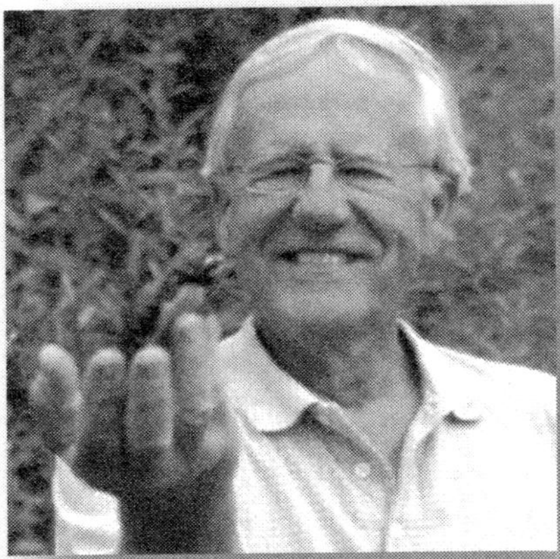
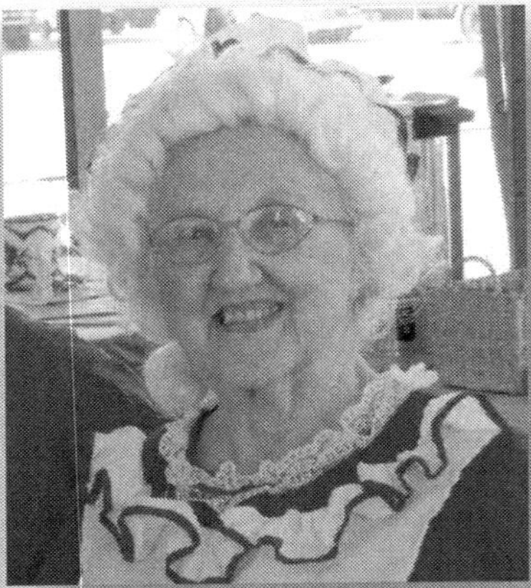
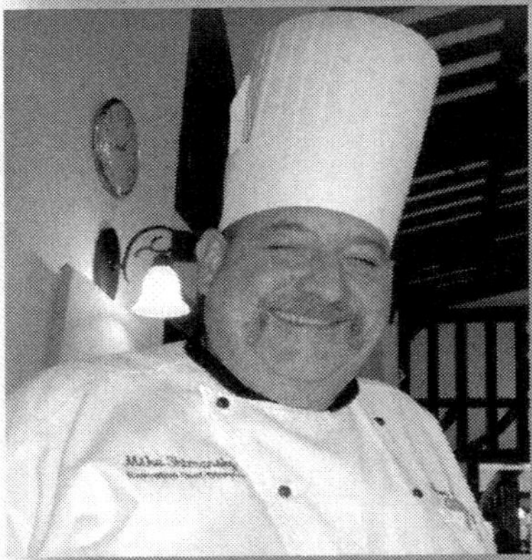
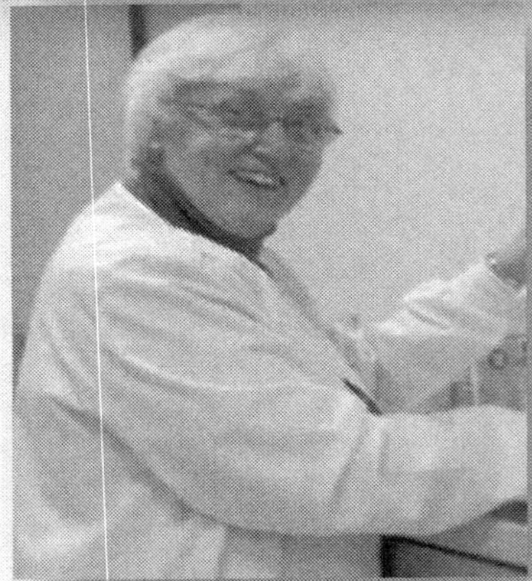
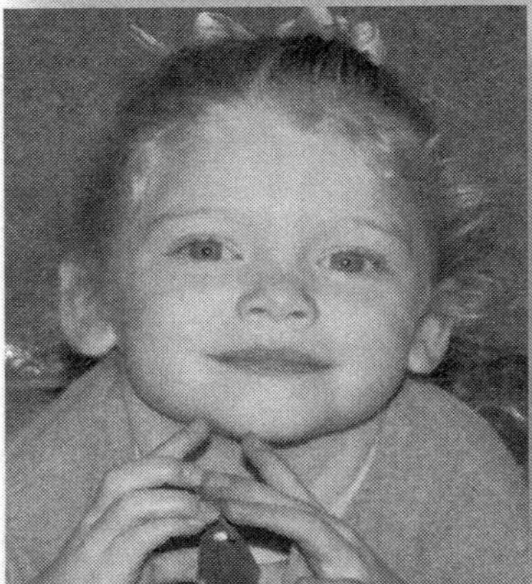
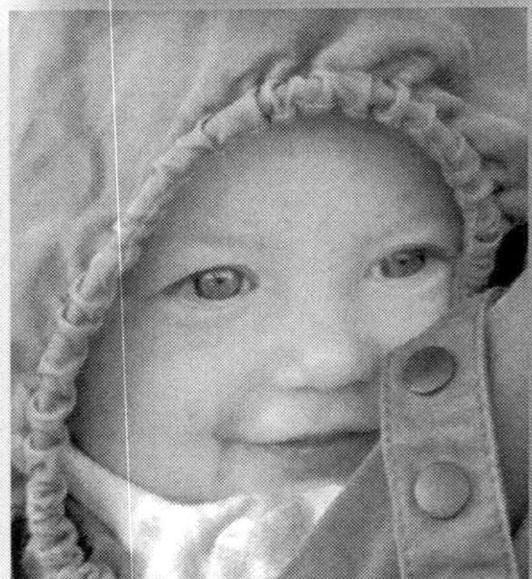

1. Now rank the rest of the photos in the order of your preference.

2. Write captions for your first three choices beginning with, "Joy is …………...

3. Which photo did you rank last, and why?

4. Which photo of an older person best represents 'joy', and why?

5. Which photo of a younger person best represents 'joy,' and why?

6. Which photo most reminds you of yourself, and why?

What Does This Tell You About Yourself?

1. "I had an easy/hard time making my choices because................

2. "I could easily imagine myself as the person in some of these photos because.........

3. "I'm usually/mostly/not a very joyful person." Explain.

4. "Thinking about being a joyful person makes me want to.....

Chapter Twenty

IS PEACE POSSIBLE?

> **Read All About It!**
>
> Read the secret of having a PEACEFUL life in Philippians 4:4-9.

Some Thoughts on Peace

Here are nine statements about peace. Read each one carefully and then summarize the main point in each statement in one sentence.

"People who look for God in the depths of their heart,
Will find a hidden quiet,
That nothing can disturb or take away.

"People who see their life as an open door,
Through which all might come to love and give again,
Will know true peace.

People who know that God has prepared them,
For a home, for all eternity, to rejoice and to be free,
Will have true peace."

(Hymn by Germaine Habjan)

"His peace he gives to us,
His peace he leaves with us,
Not for us alone,
But that we might give it again to all.

(Chorus of Hymn by M. Cecilia)

"If there is right in the soul,
There will be beauty in the person;
If there is beauty in the person,
There will be harmony in the home;
If there is harmony in the home,
There will be order in the nation;
If there is order in the nation,
There will be peace in the world."

(Chinese Proverb)

"A child is born to us!
A son is given to us!
And he will be our ruler.
He will be called, 'Wonderful Counselor,'
Almighty God,' 'Eternal Father,' Prince of Peace.'
His royal power will continue to grow;
His kingdom will always be at peace."

(Isaiah 9:6-7)

"Peace is what I leave with you;
It is my own peace that I give you.
I do not give it as the world does.
Do not be worried and upset;
Do not be afraid.

(John 14:27)

"Now that we have been put right with God through faith,
we have peace with God through our Lord Jesus Christ.
He has brought us by faith into this experience
of God's grace, in which we now live.

(Romans 5:1-2)

"The peace that Christ gives is to
guide you in the decisions you make;
for it is to this peace that God has
called you together in the one body.
And be thankful,
Christ's message in all its richness
must live in your hearts."

(Colossians 3:15-16)

"You will keep in perfect peace
those whose minds are steadfast,
because they trust in you.
Trust in the LORD forever,
for the LORD, the LORD himself, is the Rock eternal."

(Isaiah 26:3-4)

"Try to be at peace with everyone,
and try to live a holy life,
because no one will see the Lord without it."

(Hebrews 12:14)

****

Which three selections on 'peace' do you like the best, and why?

The Lifestyle of Jesus

To live peacefully, we must first of all be **at peace with ourselves**. There are many causes of inner conflict that too often rob us of that peace.

- ❖ Guilt about our past.
- ❖ Anxiety about our present.
- ❖ Worry about our future.
- ❖ Tension in our relationships with others.
- ❖ Fear of failure.
- ❖ Uncertainty about our relationship to God.

What are some of the cures for these kinds of inner conflicts?

- ❖ Experiencing forgiveness for our past.
- ❖ Experiencing faith in our present.
- ❖ Expressing hope in our future.
- ❖ Treating others as we would have them treat us.
- ❖ Having confidence in our abilities.
- ❖ Seeing failure as forgivable.
- ❖ Establishing contact with God.

To live peacefully, we must also be **at peace with our neighbors**. There are many causes of inter-personal conflict that too often rob us of that peace.

- ❖ Insisting that others accept our view of things.

- ❖ Forcing others to do what we want.

- ❖ Taking from others what doesn't belong to us (including their time and reputation).

- ❖ Being jealous of others' abilities and achievements.

- ❖ Refusing to admit it when we've wronged someone.

- ❖ Not doing what we're supposed to do and have the ability to do.

- ❖ Only being concerned with our own interests.

- ❖ Boasting of our achievements and belittling those of others.

- ❖ Speaking harshly or unkindly.

- ❖ Not being able to forgive and forget.

- ❖ Ignoring other people.

- ❖ Being disobedient to those who have a right to expect obedience.

- ❖ Being ungrateful, dishonest, crabby or impatient.

- ❖ Keeping a tight schedule and not getting enough rest.

What are some of the cures for these kinds of inter-personal conflicts?

- ❖ Developing a sense of toleration of others.

- ❖ Developing the ability to negotiate and compromise with others.

- ❖ Respecting other people's property, time and reputation.

- ❖ Celebrating other people's successes.

- ❖ Being willing to honestly confess our faults to others.

- ❖ Being responsible and dependable.

- ❖ Having as great a concern for the interests of others as we do for our own.

- ❖ Praising other people's achievements and being humble about our own.

- ❖ Turning away anger with a soft answer.

- ❖ Being ready to forgive others rather than to take revenge.

- ❖ Noticing others as much as we would like them to notice us.

- ❖ Cheerfully obeying those who rightly exercise authority over us.

- ❖ Being thankful, honest, cheerful and patient.

- Getting enough rest and keeping a sensible schedule.

To live peacefully, we must also be **at peace with God**. There are many difficulties between people and God that too often rob us of that peace.

- Trying to ignore his presence.
- Disobeying his commands.
- Refusing to admit our sin and wrongdoing.
- Forgetting to thank him for his gifts.
- Not using the abilities he gave us.
- Abusing the amazing creation he has blessed us with.
- Mistreating our neighbors.

What are some of the cures for bridging the gap between God and us?

- Believing that God exists and living as though he exists.
- Obeying his commands.
- Confessing our sins and wrongdoings.
- Thanking him in word and deed for his gifts.
- Using our God-given abilities to the fullest extent.
- Enjoying and preserving God's creation.
- Loving our neighbors as ourselves.

Peace within, with our neighbors and with God are all tied together. We can't really have one without having the other two.

Paul writes to the Christians at Colossae:

> "You are the people of God; he loved you and chose you for his own. So then, you must clothe yourselves with compassion, kindness, humility, gentleness, and patience. Be tolerant with one another and forgive one another whenever any of you has a complaint against someone else. You must forgive one another just as the Lord has forgiven you.
>
> And to all these qualities add love, which binds all things together in perfect unity. The peace that Christ gives is to guide you in the decisions you make; for it is to this peace that God has called you together in the one body. And be thankful." (Colossians. 3:12-14)

He sums it up with his final blessing to the Christians in Thessalonica. "May the Lord himself, who is our source of peace, give you peace at all times and in every way." (2 Thessalonians 3:16)

In other words, the only way to true peace within, with our neighbors and with God is to commit ourselves to believing in and living the life style of the Prince of Peace – the Lord Jesus Christ.

Jesus himself said that he is the ultimate source of our peace. "Peace is what I leave with you; it is my own peace that I give you. I do not give it as the world does. Do not be worried and upset; do not be afraid." (John 14:27)

He is the way to inner peace. "Do not be anxious about anything, but in every situation, by prayer and petition, with thanksgiving, present your requests to God. And the peace of God, which transcends all understanding, will guard your hearts and your minds in Christ Jesus." (Philippians 4:6-7)

He is the way to peace with others. "By his death on the cross Christ destroyed their enmity; by means of the cross he united both races into one body and brought them back to God. So Christ came and preached the Good News of peace to all - to you Gentiles, who were far away from God, and to the Jews, who were near to him. It is through Christ that all of us, Jews and Gentiles, are able to come in the one Spirit into the presence of the Father." (Ephesians 2:13-18)

He is the way to peace with God. "Now that we have been put right with God through faith, we have peace with God through our Lord Jesus Christ." (Romans 5:1)

Send a Telegram!

Take a piece of paper and write a 50 word or less telegram message addressed to the Secretary General of the United Nations suggesting ways of working towards world peace.

Then write a similar telegram addressed to your family or relatives suggesting ways of working towards better harmony in your family or your clan.

Finally, write a similar telegram addressed to you suggesting ways in which you could cultivate a greater measure of personal peace.

What Does This Tell You About Yourself?

1. "I feel very peaceful when ....

2. "I feel very upset when ....

3. "I do/don't feel at peace with myself because ......

4. "I do/don't feel at peace with others because……..

5. "I do/don't feel at peace with God because ....

6. "I hope that I can ....

Conclusion

You Take It from Here

So you made it to the finish line! Congratulations! But in your *real* race - the race of life - you most likely still have a ways to go. Hopefully your 'run' through this book will make that race more meaningful, purposeful and rewarding. But that's up to you. It depends on what's happened to you while reading this book - what you've discovered and what you've learned and felt about yourself and about life. By the way, just what *has* happened to you and what *have* you discovered about yourself and about life? Something? Quite a bit? A whole lot? Or nothing much? Explain.

As you look back, try to summarize your thoughts about your interaction with this book by completing each of the following in a few sentences.

1. "I've discovered that ………………………………..

2. "I've learned that ……………………………………

3. "I've felt that ………………………………………..

4. "I've decided to ……………………………………..

Now that you've wrestled with the ideas and lifestyle of Jesus Christ, how do you feel about him and his way of life? Not impressed? Impressed? Almost committed? Committed? Explain.

Suppose you were at the beach and Jesus, dripping wet from a good swim, plunked himself down on your beach mat and started a conversation. What three questions might you want to ask him and how do you suppose he might answer them?

What three questions might he ask you about yourself and how do you suppose you might answer them?

Jesus is not only interested in sharing your beach mat but in sharing your life. He said, "I have come in order that you might have life - life in all its fullness." (John 10:10) As you head into the future, why not right now (if you haven't done so already) tell him that you want to be his follower and that you want to make his lifestyle your own.

And for those of you who have committed yourself to his way of life, now is a good time to re-commit yourself to that way and to ask him to help you grow in your Christian faith and walk so that your life might become even more fulfilling and productive.

Perhaps you find the goals, the values and the ideals that Jesus modeled when he was here among us too daunting. Just remember what somebody once said: "Values are like the stars; you may not be able to reach them, but you can set your course by them."

Maria Robinson once said, "No one can go back and start a new beginning, but anyone can start today and make a new ending."

And now .... YOU TAKE IT FROM HERE!

Made in the USA
Middletown, DE
23 July 2016